RED SOX FOREVER

Books by Ellery H. Clark, Jr.

Red Sox Forever

*Boston Red Sox:
75th Anniversary History, 1901-1975*

RED SOX FOREVER

Ellery H. Clark, Jr.

Foreword by
WILLIAM C. CROWLEY,
Director of Public Relations,
Boston Red Sox

An Exposition-Banner Book
EXPOSITION PRESS
HICKSVILLE, NEW YORK

First Printing, June 1977
Second Printing, August 1977
Third Printing, March 1978

© 1977 by Ellery H. Clark, Jr.

Copyright © under the Universal Copyright
and Bern Conventions

Library of Congress Catalog Card Number: 77-78239

ISBN 0-682-48867-4

Printed in the United States of America

This Second Book

Is Dedicated To

My Loving, Loyal Wife

GRACE MARION CLARK

Founder and Artistic Director of The Annapolis Civic Ballet Company, Inc.,

Member of the General Board of the Cecchetti Council of America,

Member and Licentiate, Imperial Society of Teachers of Dancing, Classical Ballet—Cecchetti Method, London.

She was born in a year in which the Boston Red Sox were World Champions.

CONTENTS

Foreword — ix

Acknowledgments — xi

Introduction — 3

First Period: The Huntington Avenue Grounds Era, 1901-1911 — 6

Second Period: The Golden Age at Fenway Park, 1912-1918 — 29

Third Period: Frazee's Ruination of Red Sox, 1919-1923 — 49

Fourth Period: 1923-1933—Bob Quinn's Presidency a Decade of Despair — 63

Fourth Period: 1923-1933—Bob Quinn a Victim of Circumstances — 70

Fifth Period: The Yawkey Years, 1933-1976— Dedication, Enthusiasm, Money, Problems, and Three Pennants — 74

1975: A Third Yawkey Pennant — 126

Conclusions — 148

Boston Baseball Longevity — 154

Message to Boston Red Sox Fans — 162

Index — 163

FOREWORD

Ellery Clark, now sixty-seven, during the 1976 Boston Bicentennial was identified by Bob Ryan of the *Boston Globe* "as undoubtedly the greatest living authority on our Red Sox." He began his continuing interest in the Red Sox as a Boston youngster in 1918 at age 9. Even then he had the beginning of the concept which now is the central theme of this book:

> In order to produce a fine Red Sox team or teams it is necessary, in about equal amounts, to have both the individual physical and mental abilities to play the game well (he calls these the tangibles) and also team desire, dedication, unity and cooperation (these he describes as the intangibles).

For almost 60 years, Clark has maintained a close relationship with generations of Red Sox and through their fine cooperation has developed a scholarly collection of hundreds of documentary letters in response to his detailed questions on both the intangibles and tangibles. Over 70 of these letters are published for the first time and provide fascinating player insights into our Red Sox heritage.

As expected, there are some laughs, smiles and a little sadness as the author carefully identifies and evaluates the ever-changing patterns and trends of Red Sox history. Definitive, original and practical conclusions are established. It is hoped all loyal, dedicated Red Sox fans will find this volume a welcome addition to their appreciation of Boston baseball.

WILLIAM C. CROWLEY
Director of Public Relations
Boston Red Sox

ACKNOWLEDGMENTS

In the author's grateful opinion, many, many people contributed to help make his first Red Sox book, *Boston Red Sox: 75th Anniversary History, 1901-1975*, a Boston Best Seller, in 1975. Many, many people, including all those mentioned below, helped maintain the author's enthusiasm and dedication in his attempt to make the second book, *Red Sox Forever*, one that may be deserving of its title. Though a number of those whose assistance is acknowledged have passed from us, their spirit still endures.

DOCUMENTARY LETTERS:

Rick Burleson	Jim Lonborg
Bill Carrigan	Carl Mays
Jimmy Collins	Bill Monbouquette
Lou Criger	Thomas "Buck" O'Brien
Dom DiMaggio	Richard H. O'Connell
Bob Doerr	Mel Parnell
Howard Ehmke	Fred Parent
Dave "Boo" Ferriss	Rico Petrocelli
Carlton Fisk	Jim Piersall
George "Rube" Foster	Pete Runnels
Larry Gardner	Wally Schang
Norwood Gibson	Albert "Kip" Selbach
Harry Hooper	Lee Stange
Harry Hooper, Jr.	Jesse Tannehill
John Hooper	Luis Tiant
Eddie Kasko	Ted Williams

Bill Lee   Joe Wood
Edward Lewis   Carl Yastrzemski
George "Duffy" Lewis   Denton "Cy" Young

BOSTON RED SOX:

Thomas A. Yawkey
Richard H. O'Connell
William C. Crowley
Tom Dowd
Mary Jane Ryan

RELATIVES AND FRIENDS:

Tom Bates, Sports Information Director, U.S. Naval Academy
Judy Bredin
Ellery H. Clark, author's father
Victoria Mary Clark, author's mother
William E. Clark, author's son and pictorial associate
Harry Carlson, President BoSox Club
George Dearborn, Medford
Bill Gavin, South Weymouth
Janet Hobbs, Hingham
Bob Jasperson, Rosemont, Pennsylvania
Mr. and Mrs. Daniel Maddalena, author's grandparents
George Wright, Boston (Champion Boston Red Stockings, 1872-1875)
Louis Watson, Cohasset

ACADEMICIANS:

Professor Art Duhamel, *Boston Herald Advertiser*
Professor William Fowler, Northeastern University
Historian Clifford Kachline, National Baseball Library
Professor John Lucas, Penn State University
Professor Robert Moody, Boston University
Kenneth Ryder, President, Northeastern University

Professor Marshall Smelser, University of Notre Dame
Professor Ronald Smith, Penn State University
Professor David Voigt, Albright College

TV AND RADIO:

Ira Berkowitz, Channel 5, Needham
Ken Coleman, Cincinnati Broadcaster
Betty Levin, WCVB, Channel 5, Needham
John Willis, WCVB, Channel 5, Needham

NEWSPAPERS:

Harold Banks, *Boston Herald Advertiser*
Dave Bond, *South Shore News* (West Hanover)
Clark Booth, *Pilot* (Boston)
Jim Bready, *Baltimore Sun*
Bob Broeg, *St. Louis Post-Dispatch*
Roger Desjarlais, *Boston Herald Advertiser*
Wirt Gammon, *Chattanooga Times*
Al Hopkins, *Evening Capital* (Annapolis)
David Howard, *Post* (East Providence)
Phil Jackman, *Baltimore Sun*
Elmer Jackson, *Anne Arundel Times* (Annapolis)
Paul McFarlane, *Sporting News*
Lee Milazzo, *Dallas News*
Jim Murphy, *Pawtucket Times*
Harold Rich, *Bulletin* (Providence)
Ernie Roberts, *Boston Globe*
Bob Ryan, *Boston Globe*
C. C. Johnson Spink, *Sporting News*
Joe Pollack, *Sporting News*
Mark Stevens, *Christian Science Monitor*
Al Tays, *Patriot Ledger* (Quincy)

RED SOX FOREVER

INTRODUCTION

The author firmly believes it is time to take a new look at Red Sox baseball history and to give center-stage attention to a critical analysis, in which the team will be evaluated by sequential periods of history, and the continuity of patterns and trends determined. A number of pertinent inquiries will be made and conclusions provided. It is hoped that most readers will enjoy this volume and also learn the valuable lessons of past Boston baseball, which are applicable to the present and future.

Detailed, major-theme attention will be devoted equally to the accepted statistics of professional baseball *and* to the importance of the intangible factors, both of which have to be weighed and equated in order to explain why certain Red Sox teams have been more successful than others. Excerpted parts of over 70 letters to the author from Boston players, answering his detailed questions over many decades, will add documentary stature to this work. Insights, possibly fascinating, into the players' attitude toward the game, both as members of the team and as individuals, will be available. These letters cover to a degree the entire spectrum of Red Sox history, from 1901 to the present.

When General Douglas MacArthur some years ago gave his final speech at West Point, he emphasized the lifelong significance of the corps and personally regarded an army career as an enduring membership in an elite team of dedicated American servicemen. The author similarly regards the long line of Red Sox players as members of the enduring Boston team; successful or not, as their teams' records variously indicate, they will always be members of *the* team, and deserving as groups of players to be so judged and evaluated.

The author in the summer of 1976 presented, upon invitation, a special Boston Bicentennial Exhibit at Northeastern University, on whose current property was once located the original ball grounds of the Boston American League Baseball Company. The exhibit was entitled, "Early Boston American League Baseball of the Huntington Avenue Grounds Era, 1901-1911," and provided scores of photographs and other associated memorabilia from the author's personal collection. Feature writer Mark Stevens of the *Christian Science Monitor* attended the first-day luncheon and the opening of the 30-day presentation. He observed in his paper's issue of July 26, 1976:

> In letters written to Ellery Clark, author of a book based on 75 years of Red Sox history, around which the exhibit is centered, the players come across as proud of their individual accomplishments yet aware of the ball club as a team.

Thus, in analyzing the Red Sox as a team and not just as individuals, and of course paying deserved attention to the important statistics of pitching, batting and fielding as one criterion of judgment, the author holds in equal respect the team's record for 76 years to date in the intangible factors, such as were mentioned on page 163 of his *Boston Red Sox: 75th Anniversary History*. Hicksville, New York: Exposition Press, 1975:

> . . . uncomputerizable intangibles . . . in themselves are the mysterious leaven from which great performances can rise. . . . desire, confidence, consistency, achievement, close to full capability, grace under pressure, concentration, ability to face the unexpected, taking advantage of the breaks, learning quickly from mistakes, endurance . . . good team communications and cooperation, not underrating the opposition, and hustle.

One additional new approach will be to examine the major reasons why certain Boston teams, such as in 1903-1904 and 1915-1916, won back-to-back pennants, whereas the clubs of 1912, 1918, 1946, 1967 and 1975 were unable to retain their championships the next season.

The author's commitment to pay equal attention to intangibles and tangibles in evaluating the 76-year history of the Red

Sox to date is obviously a progressive approach but has some limitations. The intangibles, often involving emotions, are difficult to measure. Unlike the accepted stats of baseball, whereby the batting average of one player may be compared with that of another in the same year, the intangibles are viewed by the author through somewhat narrow (admittedly), parochial lenses, focused upon the team of his choice, Boston. He lacks the impossible ability to simultaneously recognize and evaluate the influence of these intangibles upon other American League teams.

These limitations are openly acknowledged, but even with them, a greater understanding and appreciation of the Red Sox hopefully can be reached by the reader. There is no surefire perfect formula or set of complete factors that one individual can simultaneously use to examine and determine why the American League teams have performed at various levels; why some apparently have surpassed, or just met or even fallen below their believed potential.

Hopefully, the main theme of the book as a unit, a combined image and interpretation of the Red Sox on the basis of the author's research and evaluation of selected intangibles and tangibles, may be a forward step in the published history of baseball and illustrative of the obvious and fascinating complexities associated with attempted judgments on this enduring great American sport.

FIRST PERIOD: THE HUNTINGTON AVENUE GROUNDS ERA, 1901-1911

Markedly unlike recent expansion teams in American baseball, football, basketball and hockey, the original Red Sox for various reasons got off to a fast start, being contenders in their first four seasons and winning championships twice. Ban Johnson, then League president, with financial and other assistance from such key persons as Charles Somers, Connie Mack, Hugh Duffy and Jimmy Collins, was able to put a strong team in Boston to rival and cut into the player strength and gate receipts of the Boston Nationals, who had been champions in 1897 and 1898. More than mere coincidence, the original ball field of the 1901 Boston Americans was within a good baseball's throw of the Boston Nationals' outfield. Spectators desiring to follow the new team didn't have far to go. Exchanging Boston uniforms and dedications, Collins, Freeman, Stahl and Lewis, together with the acquisition of Cy Young and Lou Criger and the signing of other key personnel, such as Bill Dinneen, pried loose from the Boston Nationals in 1902, and the shortstop-second base combination of Fred Parent and Hobe Ferris, produced a contending team from 1901 through 1904. Second in 1901 and third the next year, the team put it together in 1903.

Table 1

Year	Final Standing	Won	Lost	Net Gain or Loss In Games over Previous Season	Unofficial Pitching ERA	Team Batting
1903	1	91	47	+13½	2.57	.272
1904	1	95	59	− 4	2.12	.247

The facts, including statistical, of Boston seasons 1903-1904, are well known. These early Red Sox were experienced personnel—talented players with great determination and, with the exception of outfielder Chick Stahl's temporary injury in 1903, physically fit. With a fine infield of LaChance, Ferris, Collins and Parent, Freeman and Stahl outfield repeaters, Criger the regular catcher, and Young, Dinneen, Gibson and Winter continuing as pitchers, the club had enduring class.

The 1903 Bostons were a fine team. In winning the pennant by 15½ games, they led the League in team pitching and batting and were runners-up in fielding. Featuring three 20-game winners, Young, 28-12, Hughes, 20-7, and Dinneen, 21-13, the Boston hitters afforded great offensive support. Buck Freeman was the League's best in home runs, 13, and RBI, 104; he was ably aided by Fred Parent who drove 80 across, Jimmy Collins, 72, and Hobe Ferris, 62. Pat Dougherty was a standout in four categories: batting, hits, runs and stolen bases. In the World Series, Boston ability, confidence and depth eventually beat Pittsburg (then spelled that way), 5 games to 3, after the Pirates had taken three of the first four contests. Dinneen won three Series games, Young two. Chick Stahl, Parent, Freeman and Ferris were prominent hitters.

But not shown in any statistics, nor could they be, were certain additional contributory reasons for Boston's triumphs. As Edward Lewis's detailed *Diary* indicated for season 1901, manager-captain-third baseman Jimmy Collins was a great leader, knowledgeable of the differing moods and characteristics of individual ball players, and determined and successful in getting the most out of them, as a team. There was pride both in individual and team accomplishment. Another factor was the Bostonians' ability not to become victims of pressure, such as when they trailed the Pirates by two games in the Series. They kept their poise. As Mark Stevens also remarked about the author's Boston Bicentennial Exhibit, "The pictures displayed showed a carefree style. Players such as . . . Cy Young look earnest, but relaxed."

1904 was a true test of the team's capabilities and proved the great and continuing values of the intangibles. Dougherty, in 1904, was replaced by Selbach in the outfield and Tom Hughes by Jesse Tannehill on the pitching staff. There would be no easy 15½-game spread over the second-place club, as in the year before. By early September, the hard-driving New York team, sensing its first championship, nosed into the lead by a slim .003; but the grimly determined Sox hung on. On October 8, at the Huntington Avenue Grounds, the defending champions regained the top. The wildly partisan Boston crowd, occupying every seat and bench and overflowing in the deep outfield, cheered and applauded every offensive and defensive play of the home team. Bill Dinneen and Cy Young pitched the victories.

Two days later, at New York, the final doubleheader of the season presented the Highlanders with their last chance to dethrone Boston by a sweep, while Jimmy Collins's boys needed a split to retain the title. In the opener, Dinneen won his second game in three days, 3-2, as loser Chesbro, making his third appearance in four days, wild-pitched Lou Criger across in the ninth with Boston's decisive run.

Over the season of 1904, Boston's pitching had been superb and their fielding second-best, although the hitters dropped some 25 points to fourth in team batting. Young, 27-16, Tannehill, 21-11, Dinneen 23-14, and Gibson, 17-14, had too much proven ability and depth to be beaten. The club, despite the deceptiveness of its overall batting average, drove in runs in the clutch. Freeman drove across 84, Parent, 77, Collins and Stahl each 67, and Ferris, 63, proving that RBI are much more important than merely good batting averages. Potential runs that die on base frequently separate the losers from the winners.

IMPORTANT INTANGIBLES

Decades later, a number of the 1903-1904 Boston champions were kind enough to write the author in answer to his questions about the intangibles that contributed to their successes. A few selected excerpts from these are worth sharing with interested readers:

Jesse Tannehill to Clark, February 3, 1952

(modest Jesse did not mention his August 17, 1904, no-hitter against Chicago):

> I had good luck with that club and they won a lot of games for me. . . . they were a fine bunch.

Fred Parent to Clark, October 14, 1953

(Parent, the original Boston shortstop, played in Young's perfect game of May 5, 1904, and was over 77 when he wrote the following):

> Well, the greatest kick I have ever had was when Cy Young pitched that no hit no run game. No man reached first. The game of all time for me. What a game! I am in fine shape. Glad to hear from you.

Norwood Gibson to Clark, February 28, 1955, on the death of Bill Dinneen:

> Too bad about old Bill Dinneen. He was a good Bill and I liked him very much. He was 78 years old and next March 11, I'll be 78. We are getting old, Ellery.

Kip Selbach to Clark, January 5, 1954:

> . . . if you see Norwood Gibson, tell him 'hello'. I see Cy Young every now and then. . . . His eye sight is very bad now, you know; so he does not get to our house as often as he used to.

Tannehill, Parent, Gibson, Selbach! These late-in-life remarks prove without a doubt the lasting friendship and admiration these men felt for both the team and the various members of it. There is no doubt that the teammates' enduring spirit and attitude of comradeship, traced back to its original sources in their playing days for the first two great Boston Red Sox teams, contributed to their deserved triumphs on the ball field. May the players of today and tomorrow, and tomorrow's tomorrow, pay heed to this! Team dedication, unity, pride and cooperation are not reflected in players' salary contracts, and it is an unfailing pity they are not. These qualities are a necessity, to be contributed by individual partners in successful group achievements. In the author's judgment, they are at least of equal value when compared to the accepted statistics of baseball.

Another intangible factor in the success of great baseball teams and their individual players is their respect for worthy opponents and the added desire and determination to excel over these outstanding competitors. As Ernest Hemingway expressed it in literature, it is a moment of truth. The optimum result of course is effective concentration and maximum effort, leading to victory. For example, in the early Red Sox period, Cy Young always welcomed a mound duel with Rube Waddell of Philadelphia, knowing that it would require his very best performance, such as the 1904 no-hitter; and the next year, though he lost to the Rube in 20 innings, he did not yield a single base on balls.

Norwood Gibson was equally delighted as well as highly respectful when he faced either a great pitching opponent, such as Jack Chesbro of New York in 1904, in the year when Jack went on to set an all-time New York record of 41 seasonal wins, or the then champion batter, Larry Lajoie, in another game that same season. Had Boston lost either game, they might not have repeated as champions.

Norwood Gibson to Clark, December 18, 1953:

> Jack Chesbro was my pitching opponent and had a record of winning 14 games in a row. We [Boston] beat him in the 15th. Another thrill—we were playing Cleveland in Boston. Boston was leading 5 to 4 in 8th inning. Cleveland had men on second and third—one out. Larry Lajoie—leading the league in batting that year—came up and I said to myself, 'Oh! Oh!' Well, Larry struck out. Final score, Boston 5, Cleveland 4.

1905-1911

After the early great seasons of 1901-1904, the Boston Americans' pendulum swung the other way, as a combined consequence of having begun their team with a veteran group of experienced major-league players approaching their retirements and the inability to acquire suitable replacements. The careers of most of these Boston heroes ended between 1905 and 1908, and the team finished 4-8-7-5 respectively.

1908 marked in a very personal way the end of a Red Sox era within an era, that of the departure of Cy Young, first to Cleveland and then to the Boston Nationals, leaving his great days behind. In August, 1908, the players of the American League gave Cy a silver loving cup, in appreciation of his stature both as a man and as a pitcher. For Boston, he was a great team man and a person with whom it was a pleasure to be associated. On September 15, he gave a complimentary dinner to his Boston teammates, characteristically including the trainer and batboy. The significance is that this generous gesture of team friendship was a part of the club's success and in due time would be followed by similar team accord and admiration by the Red Sox champions of 1912, 1915 and 1916. Very important intangible assets, such as these, would be assisting influences in later great Boston baseball accomplishments.

CY YOUNG

In addition to the special cup awarded to him by all the other League players in 1908, representing the sum total of both his tangible and intangible qualities that had so stirred their admiration, the memory of Cy Young will endure in many areas, including that of the statistical records and compilations. For his Boston Red Sox career:

Table 2

AMERICAN LEAGUE SEASONAL ACHIEVEMENTS

Category	Position in Category (Number of Times)				
	1	2	3	4	5
Victories	3	1			
Shutouts	3				
Complete Games	2	1	1		1
Innings	2	1			
Strikeouts	1	2	1		1
Winning Percentage	1	1	1		1
Games	1	1			
Totals	13	7	3	0	3

Table 3

BOSTON ALL-TIME CAREER PITCHING ACHIEVEMENTS

Category	Position	Record
Innings Pitched	1	2,938⅓
Games Started	1	298
Complete Games	1	276 (.926 completion rate)
Victories	1	190
Shutouts	1	39
Strikeouts	1	1,341
Games	2	327
Winning Percentage	4	.627 (190-113)

In sharp contrast to Cy Young's very pleasant Boston experiences and memories of 1908, those of his catcher, Lou Criger, were markedly different and unhappy. Twenty years later, Lou still was upset.

Criger to Clark, dated September 10, 1928:

> I shall never forget when John I. Taylor promised a Criger day in 1908. But he failed to keep his word. I wonder if he is still the same old Taylor?

PUTNAM'S

As Bill Gavin has informed the author, many of the very early Bostons lived or roomed in the "Village," a Boston area near the Huntington Avenue Grounds and bordered by Rogers Avenue, Huntington Avenue and Ruggles Street. Chick Stahl married into a Leon Street family. But many of the players stayed at the then ball players' hotel, Putnam's, called familiarly, "Put's." As Joe Wood wrote the author, "Put's was next door to the Conservatory of Music and only 2 or 3 blocks from the old Huntington Avenue Grounds. We walked to and from the park." Hooper's letter to Clark, dated February 1, 1970, provided some interesting detailed information:

> In 09-10-11 I stayed at Putnam's as did several others. . . . Putnam's wasn't exactly a nice place but convenient. I encountered bed bugs there once. There was a dumb waiter for the second and third floors and I could order a sandwich or beer.

If the reader happens to have a copy of Clark's *Boston Red Sox: 75th Anniversary History, 1901-1975,* and if he will turn to page 47, the lower cartoon, he'll see the famous Boston Americans' horse-drawn carriage depicted. The cigar-smoking driver is a representation of the famous Pat Daley, later in charge of the player-gate on Jersey Street (renamed Yawkey Way in 1977). It appears that most of the early Bostons, except on special occasions, such as opening days, chose to walk rather than ride. But it was a promotion of the team and a thrill for area residents and others to see the horses, Pat and well-liked members of the club on their way to the park; the players responded to the waves, hellos and at least some cheers of the Boston baseball crowd. Royal Rooters also used the vehicle. But Pat Daley endured. In the words of Mr. Gavin:

> [Outside Fenway Park in later years] Pat Daley became the man in charge of the players' gate. He sat on an old wooden chair and loved to look like he was napping, but he never was. He wouldn't let his mother in unless she worked at the park. He was the grouchiest, most lovable old guy imaginable.

The St. Louis Browns generally had their troubles batting against Joe Wood, whether at home or in Boston. Recalling the summer of 1911, in St. Louis, in a letter to Clark, dated January 10, 1974, Wood writes, "I had a no hit game with 2 out in 9th inning when Burt Shotton got a single through the infield to right field. I had the no hitter on their next trip to Boston." Thus Joe, on July 29, 1911, had the honor of pitching the fourth and final no-hitter at The Huntington Avenue Grounds, joining Young, Tannehill and Dinneen of the somewhat earlier Red Sox in this achievement.

Over the first 76 years of Red Sox history, there have been 32 managers, some repeaters, such as Cronin, 13 years, Higgins, 6 years and 2 partial ones, and Bill Carrigan, two stints of 3 years each. This clearly averages out to only 2.3 years per manager, which has a number of implications. However rewarding being a manager may be, and the incumbents have had various criteria, if the team does not make at least a reasonably good showing, in the judgment of the owner and general manager, he should not be surprised if he is relieved of his duties, sometimes to become a higher up in the organization or a scout, but more often having no further connection with that club. The manager's tenure is tenuous, except under unusual circumstances, such as in Connie Mack's career of 53 years in which he survived a string of seven straight years in the cellar. If a manager also has at least a financial share of ownership, this aids his tenure.

Manager Jimmy Collins was the first Red Sox manager, from 1901 until late 1906, a well above-average length of service in view of later statistics. Club owner John I. Taylor felt that the injured Collins should be playing at third base instead of being on the sidelines and was dissatisfied with the club's rapid decline in 1905-1906. Taylor decided to remove Collins late in the season, when the team's record was a modest 44-92. Chick Stahl, the great outfielder, succeeded him as the Red Sox went on to lose a total of 105, their worst showing until 1925. Chick took his own life the next spring.

The Sporting News *reported the tragedy:*

> West Baden, Indiana. Charles S. Stahl's suicide here on March 28 shocked his teammates. . . . For some time Stahl had been using a solution of carbolic acid for a sore on his foot. He got a stone bruise and as he practiced every day, the sore didn't heal very quickly. He was given a prescription by his doctor to wash the sore with a mixture of carbolic acid and water.
>
> That's why he had the carbolic acid in his room. That's why he was able to do away with himself while his mind was unbalanced and before someone could interfere.
>
> Completely knocked out were the Boston players. They sat in the lobby of the hotel discussing the sad event, recalling Stahl's virtues and wondering how he could have done the rash act.

From then until they moved to Fenway Park in 1912, five more managers came and went; Huff, Unglaub, McGuire, Lake, and Donovan.

EARLY RED SOX WELL
REPRESENTED BY COLLEGE MEN

In the formative first years of the American League, there were relatively few men participating who earlier had been to college. But the Red Sox had an above-average number of such men, and all of them contributed much to the successes of their teams. These included the following in the Huntington Avenue Grounds Era of the Boston Americans:

Table 4

Name	College or University
Ed Lewis	Williams
Norwood Gibson	Notre Dame
Harry Lord	Bates
Bill Carrigan	Holy Cross
Harry Hooper	St. Mary's (California)
Duffy Lewis	St. Mary's (California)
Jake Stahl	Illinois
Larry Gardner	Vermont
Ray Collins	Vermont
George Winter	Gettysburg
Jimmy Collins	St. Joseph's
John Hayden	Villanova
Ambrose McConnell	Beloit

LANGUAGE CONTROL

Although only indirectly applicable to Red Sox history, but illustrating the high regard in which the commentator was held by his later 1901 Red Sox teammates, Ed Lewis in his fascinating *Diary* of his Boston baseball days provided this intimate view of one player's personal life. Lewis, also the leading pitcher in the National League for the Boston champions, in the late 1890s became a little concerned over the forceful but crude use of the spoken language by one of the best hitters and fielders of the team, and tactfully suggested the use of more socially acceptable words. Specifically, this athlete, very intense toward his performance in each game, became infuriated when he was struck out and loudly cursed the opposing pitcher as he stalked his way to the bench. Now it so happened that the player "got religion" at the same time he became engaged to a nice young lady, presumably not appreciative of his outbursts.

The player then went into a batting slump, which imperilled the progress of the club. Another member went to Lewis and complained that the player, who used to hang over the plate in commendable batting aggressiveness, now, as a prospective bridegroom thinking much of his personal safety, stood noticeably farther away to the detriment of his performance. Lewis, always the practical philosopher, looked on the bright side, pointing out that this same player now, when occasionally struck out, would return placidly to the Boston bench after having remarked, "Good Gracious."

RED SOX INDIVIDUAL LEADERS, 1905-1911

Year	Name	Notable League Achievement
1905	Tannehill, 21-9	Second in Winning Percentage, Third in Shutouts
	Young, 17-19	Second in Strikeouts, Third in ERA and Complete Games
	Ferris, .220	Second in Triples, Third in Home Runs
1907	Young, 19-15	Fourth in Complete Games, Fifth in Strikeouts
1908	Young, 21-12	Second in ERA and Complete Games, Fourth in Wins
	Gessler (RF), .308	Third in Batting
1909	Arellanes, 17-12	First in Saves, Second in Games Pitched
	Cicotte, 11-5	
	Wood, 11-8	
	Lord (3B), .311	Fourth in Stolen Bases, Fifth in Batting
	Speaker, .309	Second in Home Runs, Fourth in RBI, Fifth in Slugging Average and Total Bases
1910	Cicotte, 15-11	
	R. Collins, 14-11	
	Speaker (CF), .340	Second in Runs, Third in Batting, Slugging Average and Total Bases, Fourth in Home Runs
	J. Stahl (1B), .271	First in Home Runs, Fourth in RBI
	Lewis (LF), .283	Second in Home Runs, Third in Doubles
1911	Wood, 21-17	Second in Strikeouts, Third in ERA and Games Pitched, Fifth in Complete Games
	Pape, 13-8	
	Speaker, .327	Second in Home Runs
	Hooper (RF), .311	
	Lewis, .307	Fourth in Home Runs

PRELUDES TO VICTORY

As the preceding table to a degree indicates, the new players who in 1912 would become the World Champions were beginning to appear on the Boston playing field; Bill Carrigan and

Heinie Wagner in 1907, Tris Speaker, 1907, Joe Wood and Larry Gardner, 1908, Harry Hooper, Sea Lion Hall, Ray Collins and Steve Yerkes, all in 1909, and Duffy Lewis, 1910. Forthcoming pleasurable events cast their sunshine before, as people often discover in retrospect. This was true of the Red Sox before they moved to Fenway Park, and important intangibles would play a part in the victories that would be theirs. Some of these were: a keen desire to win and to take considered fair practice home-team advantages when opportunity offered; to anticipate developing baseball skills for a particular position they might be called upon to play; also the demonstration of off-field competitive skill and talent, which was an associate part of baseball life at least at that time. Three documentary letters comment on these points:

Harry Hooper to Clark, April 8, 1974:

I played my first year, 1909, in left field. Started in right but couldn't handle the sun. . . . But while I played left in 1909, I practiced playing the sun field until I was good at it. . . . In 1910 Duffy Lewis came up. . . . But Duffy couldn't play the sun field. So they shifted me to right and put Duffy in left. And from that day he never played any field except left. That was the beginning of the outfield Lewis-Speaker-Hooper.

Duffy Lewis to Clark, January 5, 1976:

I remember in those days of 1910 if we were behind [at the Huntington Avenue Grounds] some one on the bench would throw out a clean ball and if we were in front they would throw out a black ball for the other club to hit. . . . My first salary was 400 a month with transport to California. I was born fifty years too soon. No air conditioning in those days on railroads or hotels.

Harry Hooper to Clark, March 20, 1966

(In answer to question whom did he most admire of the early Red Sox):

I think I admired Joe Wood for his versatility. He could have starred at any position on a ball club. He was a great pool player. Good at cards and got more money out of shooting crap than he did in salary. Later a good golfer.

Interestingly, Christy Mathewson of the Giants also was very skilled at gambling and, on the whole, quite successful, according to his New York teammates.

As is common knowledge, in recent decades there have been a great many more relief pitchers used in games than formerly. In the pre-1920 years, many a pitcher, for better or worse, went the full route. Duffy Lewis looked back on the practice when he played and compared and contrasted it with recent years.

Lewis to Clark, dated January 8, 1974:

> In my day if a pitcher got knocked out of the box he went into the club house, changed his shirt and came back on the bench. Nowadays they don't come back. They go home or go out and play golf.

THE IMPORTANCE OF TURNSTILES:
PAID ATTENDANCES, 1901-1922

As post-World War II years amply have authenticated, the paid attendance figures for any professional ball club are very important, and the ratio of home parks' occupied seats to available full capacity is carefully watched. When ownership recognized a developing financial problem, established franchises were moved to new and greener playing fields. The multi-traveled Boston Braves, currently in Georgia, are a notable example.

The famous loyalty of Red Sox fans is both an intangible and tangible asset. The sustained support of their recent teams— attendances well over a million for each of the last 10 years— is the latest proof of such loyalty. Pleasingly, there was historical background and precedent for these assets as provided by the original enthusiastic Boston fans of the Huntington Avenue Grounds Era. The following statistical comparative information at first may astonish some readers, but they should take into account the influence of World War I and the beginning of the collapse of the team in the early 1920s:

1908 A POIGNANT BOSTON MEMORY. The eighth and final season at Huntington Avenue for Lou Criger and Cy Young (*upper left*). Cy started off right, achieving a swinging strike in the first pitch of the season at Boston (*lower*). On June 30, at New York, he pitched his second no-hitter for the club. In August, as shown (*upper right*), Fielder Jones presented to him a special appreciation cup on behalf of the entire American League. Young ended that year with his fifth season of 20 or more victories for Boston.

All photographs courtesy of the Ellery Clark Collection unless otherwise indicated.

MANAGER-CAPTAIN JIMMY COLLINS. Hall-of-Famer Collins piloted the club to two pennants and the 1903 World Championship. He gained and maintained outstanding universal respect from his players. He was a brilliant fielder and dependable hitter. He had great skill in keeping his men relaxed, rather than making them tension victims, in crucial games.

CHICK STAHL. An outstanding outfielder, both defensively and offensively, he relieved Collins as manager in 1906. The two men shared a number of Boston baseball records; both played on the champion Boston Nationals of 1897 and 1898 and the champion Boston Americans of 1903 and 1904. Both still stand among the Red Sox career leaders in triples: Collins, eighth, with 65, and Stahl, tenth, with 64.

OUR FIRST WORLD CHAMPION BOSTON AMERICANS, 1903! Sensing victory, the determined Bostons posed for this historic photograph just before the start of the final and decisive game against Pittsburg at the Huntington Avenue Grounds. Bill Dinneen limited the National League champions to four hits as Boston won it all, 3-0.

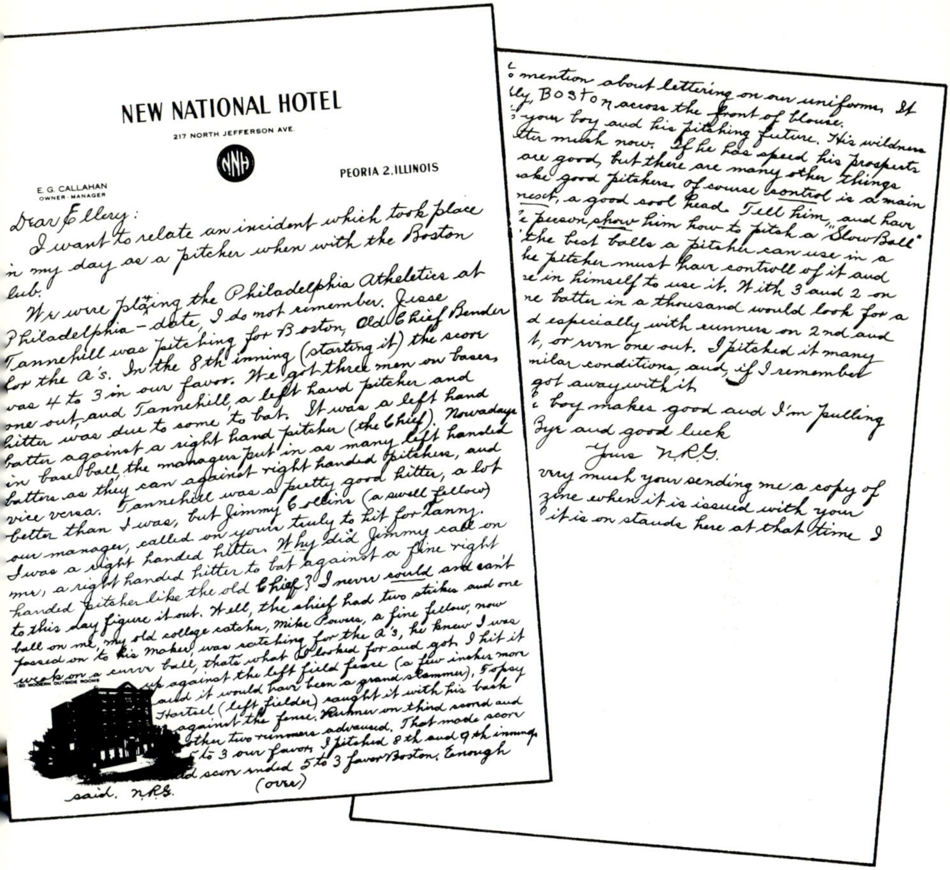

Dear Ellery:

I want to relate an incident which took place in my day as a pitcher when with the Boston club.

We were playing the Philadelphia Athletics at Philadelphia – date, I do not remember. Jesse Tannehill was pitching for Boston, Old Chief Bender for the A's. In the 8th inning (starting it) the score was 4 to 3 in our favor. We got three men on bases, one out, and Tannehill, a left hand pitcher and hitter was due to some to bat. It was a left hand batter against a right hand pitcher (the Chief). Nowadays in baseball, the managers put in as many left handed batters as they can against right handed pitchers, and vice versa. Tannehill was a pretty good hitter, a lot better than I was, but Jimmy Collins (a swell fellow) our manager, called on yours truly to hit for Tanny. I was a right handed hitter. Why did Jimmy call on me, a right handed hitter to bat against a fine right handed pitcher like the old Chief? I never could and can't to this day figure it out. Well, the chief had two strikes and one ball on me, my old college catcher, Mike Powers, a fine fellow, now passed on to his maker, was catching for the a's, he knew I was weak on a curve ball, thats what I looked for and got. I hit it up against the left field fence (a few inches more [and] it would have been a grand slammer). Topsy Hartsel (left fielder) caught it with his back against the fence. Runner on third scored and other two runners advanced. That made score [5] to 3 our favor. I pitched 8th and 9th innings [and] score ended 5 to 3 favor Boston. Enough said. N.R.G.

(over)

... mention about lettering on our uniforms, &
... ly, BOSTON across the front of blouse.
... your boy and his pitching future. His wildness
... tter much now. If he has speed his prospects
are good, but there are many other things
... ake good pitchers. of course control is a main
... nest, a good cool head. Tell him, and have
... e person, show him how to pitch a "Slow Ball"
... the best balls a pitcher can use in a
... he pitcher must have controll of it and
... re in himself to use it. With 3 and 2 on
... ne batter in a thousand would look for a
... d especially with runners on 2nd and
... t, or even one out. I pitched it many
... milar conditions, and, if I remember
... got away with it
... e boy makes good and I'm pulling
... Bye and good luck

Yours N.R.G.

... very much your sending me a copy of
... zine when it is issued with your
... it is on stands here at that time I

BOSTON NEEDED EVERY POSSIBLE WIN IN 1904. Pitcher Norwood Gibson related to the author how he, as a surprise pinch hitter, batted in an insurance run at Philadelphia and then protected the lead in relief. Gibson correctly anticipated the type of pitch Chief Bender would use. Years later, as baseball coach at the U.S. Naval Academy, Bender remembered that particular game.

EVERYBODY UP FOR BOSTON! YOU CAN DO IT, BOYS! And so the 1904 team did, vaulting into the lead over New York at Boston, October 8, 1904. (*Courtesy of the Dearborn Collection*)

BOSTON'S 1903 OR 1904 CHAMPIONS? More rather than less! Actually, this team photo was taken before the 1904 season began. Jake Stahl, Hughes and O'Brien were not on the 1904 club and two members who were, Tannehill and Selbach, are not shown. *Top row*: J. Stahl, LaChance, Ferris, Parent, Farrell. *Second row*: Young, Collins, Dinneen. *Third row*: Hughes and O'Brien. *Fourth row*: Freeman and Dougherty. *Bottom row*: Winter, Criger, C. Stahl, Gibson.

SORROWS AND JOYS OF 1906. The bad news—team finished last, with 105 defeats. Minor good news—swept this doubleheader, as the cartoon indicates. Note the details on the contour of the Huntington Avenue Grounds, including happy top-of-the-fence straddlers and eager plank-inclined walkers. The major good news? The Boston team eventually established an all-time longevity record for average life span with 74.6 years, led by Parent, 96, Young, 88, Glaze, 87, Carrigan, 85, Harris, 84, Selbach, 83, Gibson, 82, and Tannehill, 82.

JAKE STAHL. Distinguished manager and first baseman of the 1912 World Champions. Two seasons earlier, he led the League in home runs, with 10. He and his brother Chick have been the only two brothers to date in Boston baseball history to have managed the team; they did so in different years. Curiously enough, Jake and his brother, each with 16, led the club in triples, Chick in 1901 and Jake in 1910.

JOE WOOD. "Smoky Joe" still holds a number of Red Sox records, chief among them most consecutive victories, 16, in 1912, and career-best winning percentage, .663 (112-57). He stands second only to Cy Young in strikeouts, with 986, and in shutouts, with 28. Arm injuries ruined his career after a brilliant start. Joe later was identified by Harry Hooper as the most versatile Boston player of his era. Wood's blazing fastball earned him his nickname.

SHOW YOUR COLORS! OF COURSE, FOR BOSTON! In recent years of increasing collector interest and value, a vast number of in-color player cards were issued in 1908-1912. For the most part, they were distributed by such tobacco companies as Broad Leaf, Fez, Hassan, Honest Long Cut, Old Mill, Polar Bear, Piedmont, Recruit Little Cigars, Sweet Caporal and Turkey Red. Note the striking insignias on the blouses of Young and Cicotte, to this date the most colorful uniforms worn by the Boston club.

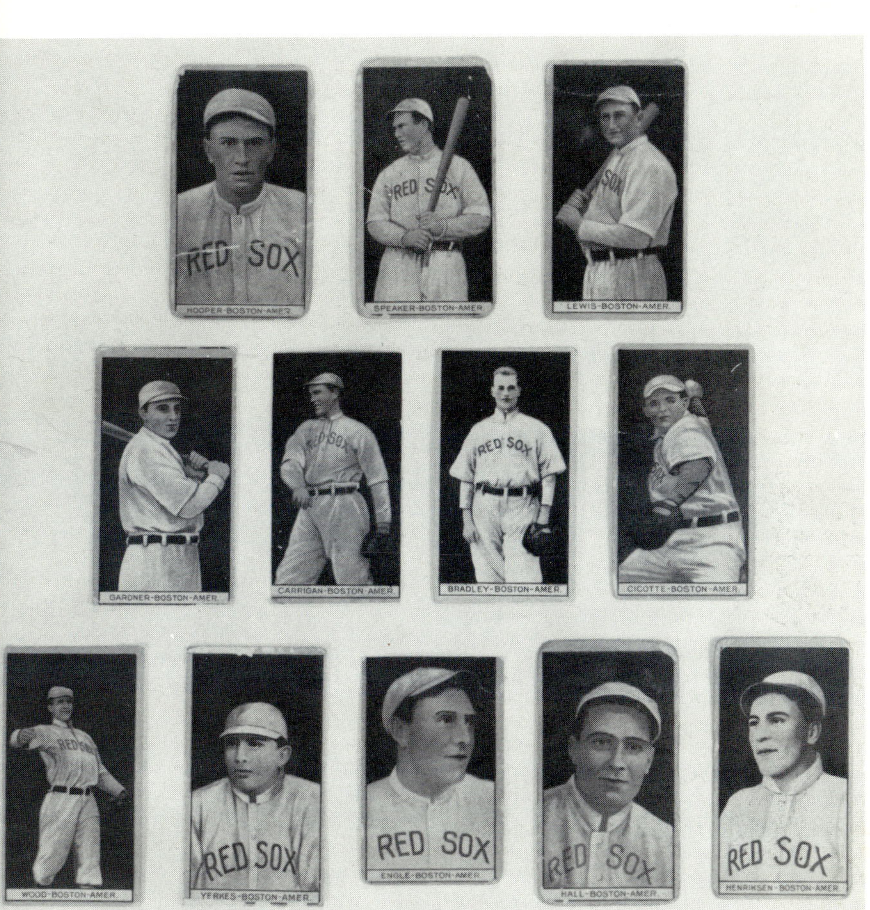

WHAT THIS COUNTRY NEEDS MOST IS A GOOD FIVE-CENT CIGAR AND A GOOD RED SOX TEAM! The best of two worlds was experienced by Boston cigar smokers of this period. Recruit Little Cigars issued a splendid 18-player set of Bostons. These Red Sox not only straddled the transition age of Boston ball parks (from Huntington Avenue to Fenway Park) but played on the 1912 World Champions. Note the all-star cast of Boston Players.

TRIS SPEAKER

TRIS SPEAKER. These views show him in the pre-Fenway period. Though his full-season Red Sox career was limited to 7 years, he still ranks in team career-leaders in 8 categories, including second in batting, .336, and second in triples, 108. Tris holds the club seasonal record for triples, 22. A salary dispute over a few thousand dollars in 1916 led to his departure to Cleveland, where for 11 years he averaged .354. This grandstand pass is obviously one of the author's Red Sox treasures.

Boston American League B.B.C.

COMPLIMENTARY

19   ADMIT ONE 11
TO GRAND STAND

TO BE TAKEN UP AT GATE

Table 5

Red Sox Home Attendance, First 11 Years,
The Huntington Avenue Grounds Era, 1901-1911

Total Attendance	5,187,055
Annual Average	471,550

Red Sox Home Attendance, Second 11 Years
(The First 11 at Fenway Park), 1912-1922

Total Attendance	4,547,493
Annual Average	413,408

THE SPEED BOYS OF HUNTINGTON AVENUE

The discerning eyes of Boston fans and reporters quickly noticed the track prowess of their early heroes, useful in many obvious ways, offensively and defensively. One of baseball's most interesting and significant categories is individual and team triples, in which the speed and frequent daring of the long-ball hitters are apparent. The top 7 Red Sox of this period in three-base hits produced a most impressive group total of 553, as follows:

Table 6

Name	Total	All-time Red Sox Position in Triples, and Total	
Speaker	97	2	(108)
Hooper	93	1	(130)
Freeman	91	3	(91)
Ferris	78	6	(78)
Jimmy Collins	65	8	(65)
Parent	65	8	(65)
Chick Stahl	64	10	(64)

Special Note: In the obviously related area of Boston career stolen bases, Hooper stands first; Speaker, second; Heinie Wagner, fourth; Gardner, fifth; Parent, sixth; Jimmy Collins, seventh; Chick Stahl, tenth. Only Yastrzemski (third) of the moderns is in the top group.

As a significant countertrend to Red Sox history of many decades, Manager Zimmer, in early 1977, has promised to transform the team into a base-stealing club. In the first 22 games of the current season, the BoSox have averaged at least one stolen base a game; indeed, on May 5, the Bostons swiped 4 bases against Seattle and repeated this feat ten days later against the same team!

PROFESSIONAL BASEBALL— A CONTRIBUTOR TO LONG LIFE?

The answer clearly is yes, especially had you been a member of the 1911 Red Sox, the last of their teams to play at Huntington Avenue. They took with them and later maintained and extended a remarkable ability to achieve longevity. The Athletics won both of baseball's titles that season, but over the eventual years, in the longevity league, the Boston Red Sox would be World Champions. The proof:

Table 7

Name	Position, 1911	Age (* Indicates alive in 1977)
Nagle	P	91
Lewis	LF	89*
Gardner	3B-2B	89
McHale	P	88*
Wood	P	87*
Hooper	OF	87
Riggert	OF	86
Gunning	1B	86
Carrigan	C	85
Baker	1B	85
Cicotte	P	84
Ray Collins	P	82
Yerkes	SS	82
Killilay	P	81

Special Note: By interesting coincidence, all 9 positions are represented and 6 of the 14 were pitchers. Perhaps the fountain of youth existed at the original ball park, but there are rumors that it may exist in Florida.

SECOND PERIOD: THE GOLDEN AGE AT FENWAY PARK, 1912-1918

Table 8

Year	Final Standing	Won	Lost	Net Gain or Loss in Games Over Previous Season	Pitching ERA	Team Batting
1911	5	78	75	− 3	2.73	.274
1912	1	105	47	+27½	2.76	.277
1913	4	79	71	−25	2.94	.269

1912 AND 1913 SEASONS

In 1911, although Red Sox pitching was the best in the league, the Athletics ran away with the pennant by 13½ games, 24 ahead of Boston, chiefly because they topped the other clubs in batting with a robust .296. Philadelphia's pitchers also were supported by good pitching and the best fielders. But the Red Sox were ready in 1912 and set a new American League victory mark of 105 that would last for 15 years. The club's all-around power was indicated by the statistics: second in team pitching, batting and fielding. "Smoky" Joe Wood set an all-time Boston seasonal record of 34-5, ably assisted by Buck O'Brien with 19 wins, Hugh Bedient, 18, and Ray Collins and Sea Lion Hall, each with 15. Delivering run-scoring hits when needed, the Bostons outscored their rivals by 256 runs, as their RBI group was headed by Duffy Lewis, with 109, Tris Speaker, 90, Larry Gardner, 86, Heinie Wagner, 68, Manager Jake Stahl, 60, and Harry Hooper 53.

INVENTIVENESS OF EARLY RED SOX

Although practice is no guarantee of perfection, Duffy Lewis was quick to realize the new problem at Fenway Park in left field, which made chasing flies quite unlike his earlier outfielding experience at the Huntington Avenue Grounds. In the same spirit with which Harry Hooper had prepared himself to play the difficult right field, Duffy, in his first practice at the then new Fenway Park, appraised the geographic difficulties of the miniature cliff in left field and then took action:

Duffy Lewis to Clark, February 1, 1976:

> About 'Duffy's Cliff' [ultimately named in his honor for his skill in playing it], I used to go out and practice in the morning. You had to take one look at the ball. Go up if you had a chance to get it. You couldn't keep looking at the ball. If you did, down you went when you hit the bank.

It sometimes is difficult to see the forest for the trees. The author is convinced that a highly important intangible asset of ball players, perhaps truer of the old-timers than the newer breed, is that of inventiveness, which in itself is the child of desire, as well as of necessity. Hooper and Lewis, as each recounted in the extracts, had this most desirable quality, which illustrated the degree of attention and concentration they placed upon their profession. The author, for example, though only a young boy in 1918, remembers very well the sliding catches Hooper used to make in right field. Coming in on a short fly, he would slide on his knee the last few yards and achieve at least two goals. If he caught the ball, he would be in a good position to regain his footing and complete a double play if the base runner had incorrectly anticipated a safe hit; if he did not catch the ball, it would most likely strike him in the chest, or other forward area, and he still would be in a fine position to recover the ball, perhaps to throw out an advancing runner who thereby would be the victim of Hooper's carefully considered, planned and executed defensive play.

Thus, considerable intangible ability and usefulness to the team were demonstrated by Hooper on many an occasion, and often it at least partially showed in the statistics of baseball— the mounting totals of assists with which he was credited each season.

Perhaps a half-credit for the intangibles also should be scored for the durability of many players, in part reflecting their determination to play if at all physically possible. Kip Selbach wrote the author on January 5, 1954: "I played in every inning of every game played, unless I was hurt." The Red Sox of 1910-1915, counting games played to a decision, had a total of 912. For the same period, Speaker participated in 884, Lewis, 882, and Hooper, 870. The outfield equates to 96.3 percent of these games. Desire and determination to play were trademarks of early Bostons and many others; that such zeal is not restricted to time capsules is evidenced by Boston's present captain, Carl Yastrzemski.

FAMOUS WOOD-JOHNSON DUEL, 1912

Obviously, many ball players are very happy in later years to select and recall a particularly thrilling moment of their active career. On September 6, 1912, at Fenway Park, Walter Johnson, who earlier had won 16 straight (from July 3 to August 26), faced Boston's Joe Wood, who was working on his own streak of 14 in a row (Joe extended his streak to 16). Red Sox fans packed the park and the production was equal to the promotion of the duel. Sixty-two years later, Duffy Lewis summarized:

Lewis to Clark, dated January 8, 1974:

> The most thrilling game was the Joe Wood-Walter Johnson game. Speaker doubled and I doubled. We won, 1 to 0.

1912 WORLD SERIES

As the 1912 World Series approached, the contestants appeared evenly matched. Both had won easily, the Giants by 10 games, Boston by 14. New York had just won their second straight pennant, leading their league in pitching and batting for both campaigns. Mathewson, 23-12, Marquard, 27-11, and Tesrau, 16-7, were ably supported by Chief Meyers, .358, Larry Doyle, .330, and Fred Merkle, .309. Boston also had three regulars over .300: Speaker, .383, Gardner, .313, and Stahl, .301.

What followed was an amazing Series, well worth commentary even after 65 years. Excitement, rapid turnabout in fortunes, crucial catches, errors and hits, and the Sox coming back from probable defeat led Harry Hooper to write the author many decades later, the image and significances of the final game still fresh and enduring in his intelligent mind: "The joy and jubilation we experienced at winning after it looked as if we were going to lose cannot be expressed in words."

Another intangible factor, frequently present in organized athletics, is tension. In a perceptive 1965 letter to Clark, Harry Hooper commented on this subject as it was related to the 1912 World Series:

> Judging from the newspapers before the season, Wood had to do all the pitching. . . . Joe [in the season] had just finished a string of 16 straight games [victories]. All those games after the first 5 or 6 were under tension. A pitching duel was advertised in each town with their best pitcher. The following build up for the Series put extreme tension on Joe. And it had its effect. Joe won three games, but he wasn't pitching like he was in the regular season. In the 7th game we figured we would win with Joe and end it. Just as he was warming up, the game was delayed for probably 10 minutes. I ran in to chat with Joe who was still throwing easily in his warmup. I tried to converse with him, but he was so tense, he never said a word. The game was gone before we could get the first three men out. That is when my tension left me.

Earlier, at the start of the Series, as Hooper wrote the author many years after:

> The tension was great before the first game [in New York] of our first Series. I remember Gardner and I (rooming together) started talking about the game in the middle of the night.

The tension and lack of sleep the night before apparently did not lessen Hooper's performance the next day in the first game; he doubled home Wagner and Wood, then scored what proved to be Boston's winning run, all in the top of the seventh inning.

The Red Sox took the opener at New York, 4-3, Wood being superior to Tesrau. Joe later commented in a letter to the author that this was his greatest thrill in a World Series because:

> . . . we were leading by one run, last of 9th, one out and Giants on second and third. . . . For the second out I struck out Art Fletcher and then McGraw sent in Doc Crandall, who had never struck out at the Polo Grounds. His strike out was the final out.

The second, at Boston, was a 6-6, 11-inning tie, ended by darkness, in which the Red Sox tied the game in the last of the tenth, and their combined pitching of Collins, Hall and Bedient, plus five Giants' errors, held Mathewson to a draw. In the third game, Josh Devore's great catch in the last of the ninth preserved a 2-1 New York lead, with Marquard nosing out O'Brien and Bedient. The Red Sox won the fourth at New York, 3-1, beating Tesrau a second time. When Bedient trimmed Mathewson 2-1, also at New York, on triples by Hooper and Yerkes followed by Doyle's error, the Bostons were on the verge of victory. But Manager Stahl's recommendation to start Wood in the sixth game was vetoed by club owner McAleer, and O'Brien, who had done well, though losing the third game, was sent to the mound. He lasted one inning, yielding six hits, one balk and five runs as the Giants prevailed, 5-2. Returning to Boston for the final game, or games, Joe Wood, bidding for his third win, instead had a disastrous first inning as the New Yorkers pounded him for 7 hits and 6 runs, romping to an 11-4 Series-tying victory. Boston pessimists feared the worst in the deciding game, and, curiously, many discouraged fans stayed away from what would be one of the most thrilling Series games of all time.

Mathewson, seeking his first 1912 Series victory, started and went all the way, with Bedient opposing him for the first 7 innings. But the game-mosaic was one of extraordinary influences

and events, culminating in the most exciting Boston World Series
victory to date. Hooper's finding of the Catholic prayer card at
the start of the game, his marvelous catch off Doyle in the top
of the sixth, which held the New York lead to 1-0, Olaf Henricksen's game-tying pinch double in the seventh and finally, after
the Giants went ahead in the top of the tenth, the combination
of Snodgrass's and Merkle's errors, Speaker's hit and Gardner's
winning sacrifice fly pulled it out for the Red Sox, 3-2. *Reach's
1913 Official American League Guide* concluded their review of
the Series by observing, "And so ended the most desperately
contested World's Series on record."

According to the continuing thoughts, wonderment, and conclusions of Harry Hooper, the influence of Jesus well may have
led to Boston victory. It was a very cold comfort for the Giants
that they had won much of the battle of statistics over the Red
Sox: better ERA, higher team batting, more runs, more hits, more
walks. The New Yorkers would have to wait another nine years
for a World Championship; the Red Sox would wait only three.
It was good that the Boston team and fans were especially happy
at the end of the 1912 Series. 1913 would prove to be different.

1913 SEASON

In 1913, the team finished fourth, 25 games behind the champion Athletics who during 1910-1914 would win four pennants,
three World Championships and achieve an annual average of
97 victories. The major cause of the Red Sox's not doing better
was Joe Wood's broken hand, suffered early in the season.
Whereas the year before he had appeared in 344 innings and
attained a 34-5 record, in 1913 he was able to pitch only 144
innings and had a 9-5 season. His net loss of 25 victories exactly
matched the number of games the team finished behind Philadelphia. O'Brien, who had won 19 the year before and was not
particularly liked by owner McAleer, was transferred to Chicago
after an early season record of 4-7. The still very vocal Buck,
years later recalling the incident to the author, remarked, "Good
God! They might just as well have shipped me to Hawaii!"

Manager and first baseman Jake Stahl (he and brother Chick are the only brothers to have managed the Red Sox) was injured and played in only a couple of games, not batting in a run, in contrast to his pennant year total of 60. Friction developed and McAleer, upset by rumors that Stahl would like to buy the club, dismissed him in July, selecting Bill Carrigan as managerial replacement.

But the 1913 setback was only temporary, as Red Sox clubs of 1912 through 1918 would prove to be the sustained best in their 76-year history to date. Four pennants, four World Championships and a pair of second-place finishes would be their record. The problems of 1913 were also mitigated by Lewis-Speaker-Hooper's setting an American League seasonal outfield record of 84 assists, and the appearance of George Foster and Dutch Leonard, soon to be pitching stars.

1914 SEASON

That season found the Red Sox with a good team, winning 91 games, but still second, 8½ games behind Connie Mack's Athletics. The Philadelphians went on to lose four straight to the Boston Braves in the World Series, then collapse for seven consecutive years in the cellar. The 1914 Red Sox had the best pitching but were second in fielding and third in batting, as the Athletics finished first in batting and fielding and fourth in pitching. Comparatively, the A's outhit Boston by 22 points and had three men in the top five RBI producers.

For the Red Sox, Tris Speaker had a tremendous season, .338, and placed first in League total bases, hits and doubles, and third in batting, RBI, runs, triples and stolen bases. Hoblitzell batted .319, while Ray Collins, 20-13, Dutch Leonard, 18-5, Rube Foster, 14-8, and Ernie Shore, 10-4, were a strong corps. Newcomer Babe Ruth appeared in four games. When the breakup of the Athletics began after the 1914 season, the Red Sox were ready to take over, and manager Bill Carrigan, with a full season of leadership under his belt, was prepared to urge and drive the club to the top, particularly since he knew the team's abilities and potentials.

1915 AND 1916 SEASONS

Table 9

Year	Standing	Won	Lost	Net Gain or Loss in Games Over Previous Season	Team ERA	Team Batting
1914	2	91	62	+10½	2.35	.250
1915	1	101	50	+11½	2.39	.268
1916	1	91	63	−11½	2.48	.248

The Red Sox clubs of 1915 and 1916 had to be good to win, since Detroit finished only 2½ behind the first year and Chicago only by 2 the next. Meanwhile, in those two seasons, the Athletics managed to lose 226. All-around great Boston balance was indicated by the stats: in 1915, second in pitching and batting, third in fielding; and in 1916, second in pitching, first in fielding, and fourth in batting (Speaker had been dealt to Cleveland).

As in 1904 and 1905, one reason for Boston's continuing success was a competitive, talented, cooperative and experienced team, leavened by two great newcomers, Ruth and Mays. Hoblitzell was at first, Gardner at third, Everett Scott, shortstop, Lewis in left, Hooper in right, and Thomas and Cady the catchers. A great mound staff carried them through. In 1915, Rube Foster, Ernie Shore, Babe Ruth and Dutch Leonard compiled a 70-31 record, and the next year went 70-41. In total wins for the two campaigns, Ruth had 41 and Foster, Leonard and Shore each 33. Mays's 19-13 record in 1916 compensated for the loss of Wood, who had been 15-5 the year before.

LEWIS NOW BATTING FOR RUTH!

When Duffy Lewis put on his uniform for the game of July 11, 1914, at Fenway against Cleveland, little did he think that he was about to make baseball history, especially in view of later events. On that date, Babe Ruth made his first start for Boston. As he weakened on the mound in late innings, Manager Carrigan cast a thoughtful eye down his bench for a likely pinch hitter. Lewis recounted the conversation 60 years later.

Lewis to Clark, dated January 8, 1974:

> I had been out of the lineup for a week with a sprained ankle. Bill Carrigan said to me, 'Can you hit?' I said, 'Sure!' 'Hit for Ruth,' he replied. I got a hit.

Babe Ruth, as full of pranks as a healthy bear cub, and possessed of a very carefree attitude toward Manager Carrigan's rules and regulations of conduct and discipline, contributed outstanding pitching to the Boston cause in 1915 and 1916. In the earlier year, he was 18-8, finishing fourth in League winning percentage, behind three teammates, Wood, Foster and Shore. The next season, he blossomed into extensive League prominence, going 23-12. He was the leader both in ERA and shutouts, second in victories, third in winning percentage, innings pitched and strikeouts, and fourth in complete games. Whereas in 1915, Manager Carrigan, deep in experienced pitchers for the World Series, did not use the Babe, in 1916, Ruth won his single appearance, a 14-inning game, and began his eventual record streak of consecutive scoreless Series innings. He also was the leading Series pitcher in ERA. Ruth was a very durable pitcher for his Boston career, 1914-1919, starting 143 games and going the distance in 105 of these, for a complete games percentage of .735.

In 1915-1916, batting as a pitcher, Ruth provided intimations of his future greatness as a hitter and slugger. In these regular seasons, combined, he hit for a very respectable .289 (66 hits in 228 appearances). In the 1916 Series, in five plate appearances he failed to make a hit. By 1918, the conversion of Ruth would begin, at which time he would appear as a pitcher in only 20 games in contrast to his use in the outfield in 59 and at first in another 13.

MANAGER BILL CARRIGAN

Bill Carrigan deserved special credit for the second Boston pennant double and two consecutive World Championships. Bill Carrigan, whose letters generally were much briefer than his clubhouse meetings, had no problem selecting his most pleasant recollection with the Red Sox.

Carrigan to Clark, dated May 24, 1955:

> I will say that my happiest memory as a Red Sox was being manager in 1915 and 1916 and winning the pennant and World Series each time.

Hooper in a long letter to Clark, January 17, 1974, paid a splendid tribute to Carrigan:

> He was a great catcher. With a weak arm he would get his throw away so quickly that even Cobb had trouble stealing against him. Bill was also the greatest in getting the most out of his pitchers. When pitchers would get into a slump, Bill would put on the catcher's togs and catch to straighten the pitcher out. On two occasions [in 1916] he caught pitchers who were in a slump and they pitched no hitters when he caught them [Leonard and Foster].
> I think Bill was the best manager I played for. A great manager can get the most out of a good team, but if he doesn't have the material [the horses] he cannot win.

Typical of Carrigan's successful approach, in 1915, when the club arrived in Detroit for an important series and had to face a nemesis, George Dauss, in the opener, Bill asked for a volunteer to go out and pitch a victory. Carl Mays put his hand up and stated that if he did not win, he would walk all the way back to Boston. Mays returned with the team by train after the road trip, having won his game, 2-1.

LEWIS-HOOPER-SPEAKER, 1910-1915

Baseball seasons have their own joys and sadnesses. 1915 proved to be the sixth and last year of the greatest defensive outfield in the history of major-league baseball. During these seasons, Lewis, Speaker and Hooper made a total of 455 assists, with Speaker achieving 161, Hooper 150 and Lewis 144, in addition to their spectacular catches. In Duffy Lewis's letter to Clark of February 1, 1976, he revealed many of the secrets and explanations for their success:

> The outfield of Hooper, Speaker and Lewis was pretty good according to a number of people. Tris Speaker was the king of the outfield. If a player hit mostly to left field he would move Hooper over from right. It was the same moving around on every player. It was always 'Take it,' or 'I got it.' In all the years we never bumped each other. We all had good arms. Ty Cobb knew it. Many a time he tried to make a double on a single but we got him many times. . . . I always liked to play against Detroit to see Cobb operate. He was something to watch. I remember many times that Cobb would come out after the second hitter. No batting practice. Here comes Cobb. If he wasn't hitting he would be bunting his way on. The best in the business.

The departure of Speaker to Cleveland after the 1915 season is a significant story, typical of those times. Red Sox owner Joe Lannin was dissatisfied with Speaker's performance, such as his batting decline in the past three seasons from .383 to .338 to .322. Joe Wood also felt Lannin's displeasure. Speaker was outraged at the prospect of having his potential salary reduced by one-half, which would have put him under $10,000. Wood was offered $5,000. In those days, there were no players' rights, agents or bargaining. Lannin's attitude was in keeping with the bad-ogre profile of owners when salary differences developed. Thus, refusal to accept proffered cuts brought about Lannin's reprisals, one immediate the other delayed. Tris was dealt to the happy Clevelanders, and Wood, who became a 1916 holdout, was sold to the Indians the following winter.

In retrospect, Lannin could not and would not compromise or otherwise give in to player demands. Thus, for an amount less than $10,000, Lannin provided Cleveland with his star player, who in eleven brilliant seasons for them would make 1965 hits in 5547 official times at bat for a career average of .354. Had Lannin met Speaker's demand, it seems logical to assume that by the time of the hard-pressed Frazee regime, and quite possibly in 1920, Tris would have gone to the player-hungry Yankees, along with the other Boston stars who actually did.

Hooper, in another letter to the author, effectively indicated the competitive spirit of the 1915 Red Sox and their intention as well as ability to use all their strengths to advantage:

> I think our 1915 team was one of the greatest teams in baseball, with the best pitching staff and the best defensive outfield. We played for one run—tried to get on the scoreboard first and then to increase our lead.

Another indication of the Boston greatness in 1915 and 1916 was their granted right and ability to make player decisions on the spot, without benefit of coaches' signs. For example, in Lewis's letter of February 1, 1976, to Clark:

> In my day we did not have to look at third base to see what to do. We did everything by ourselves. Put on hit and run, double steal and squeeze play.

In general, one may argue about this practice, at least from a later-day point of view, and the at least supposed advantages in discerning stop or go situations that first- and third-base coaches should have. But on the other hand, given a group of talented and experienced players completely dedicated to winning and knowing their opponents quite thoroughly, it seems these early Red Sox did the right thing. Certainly, their achieved records are difficult to dispute. Their dedicated concentration on the game as a group probably separates them very noticeably from the teams of today, with very few exceptions.

GEORGE "RUBE" FOSTER (1913-1917)

A man of many baseball talents, Foster was a .275 career-hitting pitcher for the Red Sox, his only major-league club; he compiled a 58-34 record, including a June 21, 1916, no-hitter against New York, two World Series wins in 1915 and 16 Boston shutouts. As is typical of intelligent, inquiring pitchers he was the inventive sort.

Foster to Clark, dated August 5, 1955:

> You know, that unless you want to call Christy Mathewson's fadeaway a screw ball, I invented the screw ball and used it at Boston 5 years before any other pitcher used it. Also, the hesitation pitch of Satchel Paige's fame. I had to stop using that because Tommy Connolly and Billy Evans called balks on me. Of course in those days we got no high powering press agent and radio build up. Do you have a record of how many shutouts I pitched for Boston?

HAPPY FAMILY

Another intangible asset these Bostons had was very well expressed by Larry Gardner, in a letter to Clark of May 10, 1974:

> In fact the whole experience was very pleasant and interesting. It was like a big happy family. . . . I don't believe the players today have that happy experience.

In the continued wranglings over long-term, very lucrative contracts in 1976 and 1977, there is no doubt that the almost amateur spirit of dedication and concentration of past baseball most unfortunately is probably extinct. The old-time players were far less shrewd, far less concerned about their financial futures than the businessmen-athletes of today.

WORLD SERIES OF 1915 AND 1916

The Series of 1915 and 1916 are deserving of special mention because the Red Sox proved their expertness and proficiency without any lingering doubts. In the first Series, Philadelphia was beaten in 5 games, while the next one saw the Brooklyn Dodgers suffering the same one-sided fate. Boston pitching, plus timely hitting, was the answer. Combining these two Series, we find seven of the ten games were decided by a single run, Boston winning four of five from the Phillies by this margin and taking two of the three one-runners from the Dodgers.

Some condensed stats indicate Boston's superiority:

Table 10

1915	Team Pitching ERA	Team Batting	RBI	Pitchers' Complete Games
Red Sox	1.84	.264	11	5
Phillies	2.27	.182	9	4
1916				
Red Sox	1.47	.238	18	3
Dodgers	2.85	.200	11	1

In the 1915 Series, Foster won two, Leonard and Shore each one, as they were the only three Boston pitchers required and each went the full route. In 1916, Shore won a pair, Ruth and Leonard one each.

Duffy Lewis was the batting star of the two Series, at .444 in 1915 and at .353 in 1916, for a combined 14 hits in 35 appearances for .400. Lewis, for all his admitted love of the game for its own sake, appreciated the additional World Series money as a twice-in-a-row champion; the purse totaled $7,690.51 for the ten games. Duffy later wrote the author, "The 1915 World Series was my best because after the series I went into vaudeville [Pantages Theater] and made a couple of thousand dollars."

"IT'S NOT ONLY WHAT YOU DO BUT WHERE YOU DO IT THAT COUNTS"

Few would disagree with this truism. he 1915 World Series emphasized the point at least four times. Had it not been for the temporary seats in Baker Field's center field, Hooper would not have had his two home runs. In games three and four, both played in spacious Braves Field, Boston. Duffy Lewis was able to haul down two long drives, one in each game, by Philly's Gabby Cravath. After that Series, Lewis appeared in vaudeville in Los Angeles, Cravath's home town.

Undated Letter of Lewis to Clark:

I opened in San Francisco then Oakland, Los Angeles and San Diego. In Los Angeles a man asked me in what park did you make that catch off Cravath. I told him it was Braves Field. He said that was a big field, wasn't it. I said yes. Baker Bowl was the name of the Phillies Park. Very small park. He said if he [Cravath] hit that ball in Baker Bowl he would be doing the act instead of you. I had a lot of fun.

Lewis and Hooper apparently were determined not to have the World Series go beyond 5 games that year. In that fifth game, between them they contributed 3 home runs, a very unusual accomplishment in the dead-ball era. Hooper had 2 of them and in each case the ball struck the outfield grass, then bounded into the temporary center field seats of the Phillies' stadium. Much later on, Hooper was not pleased at Fred Lieb's referring to them as "Chinese homers." Lewis's recollection is brief and to the point.

Lewis to Clark, dated January 8, 1974:

> In the 1915 Series I won two games, beating Alexander, 2-1 and George Chalmers, 2-1. In the last game . . . I hit a home run off E. J. Rixey, one man on and two runs behind . . . Hooper next inning hit a home run [his first had come in the third] winning the game, 5 to 4.

1917-1919 SEASONS

Table 11

Year	Position	Won	Lost	Net Gain or Loss in Games Over Previous Season	Team ERA	Team Batting
1917	2	90	62	—	2.20	.246
1918	1	75	51	+ 2	2.31	.249
1919	6	66	71	−14½	3.30	.261*

*1919 was the first year of the lively ball. League total home runs leaped from 100 in 1918 to 240 in 1919.

For a variety of reasons, these three seasons were very critical in Boston baseball history, as the Red Sox in 1918 again reached the top, including both League and World Championships, for the fourth time in seven years. But, beginning in 1919, the adverse influences of owner Harry Frazee began to undermine and then to destroy the club. In his first two years as owner, the team finished second and first, respectively, as Frazee did his best. But from the conclusion of season 1919 to the end of his ruinous control in 1923, Harry's floundering finances, under the impact of generally failing musical comedies and heavy mortgage and interest payments on his baseball property, forced him to sell a long line of Red Sox stars to the New York Yankees, starting both Boston's long and sustained plunge to the bottom of the League and, concurrently, the rise and dominance of the New York club.

In 1917, the Red Sox put up a very good fight for a third consecutive pennant. Under new manager Jack Barry, who also played second base, the club won 90 games. But the White Sox won 100, largely due to the unbeatable combination of a fine, deep pitching staff, including former Boston pitcher Eddie Cicotte (28-12); the ability in late innings to maintain early leads; and timely hitting. Brilliant Boston pitching by Carl Mays, 22-9, and Babe Ruth, 24-13, suggested to Frazee and Barry the good possibility of winning the next year, provided suitable replacements could be obtained for the Bostons who had left or soon would leave to join the American wartime armed forces. These would include Barry, Hoblitzell, Janvrin, Lewis and Shore.

Frazee thereupon acquired from Connie Mack four of his veterans: first baseman Stuffy McInnis, outfielder Amos Strunk, pitcher Joe Bush and catcher Wally Schang. From Cincinnati came second baseman Dave Shean, and from the minors veteran George Whiteman, who would play the outfield for Boston when Ruth pitched. These new players, together with holdovers Everett Scott, shortstop, Harry Hooper, right field, and pitchers Ruth and Mays, appeared capable enough to win.

And so they did, nosing out Cleveland by 2½ games. As a team, the Boston posture was erratic: first in fielding, second in ERA and sixth in batting. The Red Sox were difficult to score on, as McInnis, Scott and Strunk led the League in their positions, while Hooper was best in right-fielder double plays. Four pitchers performed nobly: Mays, 21-13, Sad Sam Jones, 16-5, Ruth, 13-7, and Joe Bush, 15-15, the latter's record enhanced by his being among the League leaders in four pitching departments. Jones was best in winning percentage, and Mays tied for first in complete games. Ruth, serving double-duty as outfielder-pitcher, hit .300 with 66 RBI and 11 home runs in 95 games, while McInnis batted across 56 runners. Hooper had another banner season: second in League doubles and triples, third in walks and runs. Shean, Strunk and Whiteman all had good regular campaigns in this abbreviated wartime schedule, in which the Red Sox played 126 games to decisions. The *1919 Reach Guide* indicated the main reasons for Boston's triumph: "With airtight defense and great pitching . . . the Red Sox played a brand of ball which more than compensated for their lack of team batting strength. Schang and Agnew gave the pitchers excellent support."

1918 WORLD SERIES

This Series was remarkable for a number of reasons, including the fact that it would be the last Series triumph for Boston to the present time, 1977. Also, a player strike would seemingly be settled with no reprisals on the players, only to develop into an unhonored alleged promise, according to Hooper, and the subsequent refusal of baseball commissioners to award the usual World Series championship emblems to the winning Bostons. In addition, the Series would prove a miniature of the Red Sox' regular season performance, leading the *1919 Reach Guide* to observe, "Superior pitching and . . . airtight fielding, and the Red Sox hung up a World Series record for fielding efficiency, as but 1 error was marked up against them in 6 games."

Boston beat Chicago's Cubs, 4 games to 2, as each Red Sox victory was by a single run; Ruth prevailed, 1-0 and 3-2, while Mays twice triumphed by 2-1. The Cubs won the war of statistics, with a better ERA and batting average than their opponents, more runs and RBI. With the exception of Bush relieving winning pitcher Ruth in the ninth inning of the fourth game, every Boston starter went the full route. In addition, the Babe extended his consecutive scoreless inning streak to 29⅔ innings, a new record, before the Cubs scored on him.

George Whiteman, who did well at bat and was brilliant in the field for the Red Sox, was selected the hero of the Series. One of his defensive gems, in the eighth inning of the final game, received this description in *Reach's Guide:*

> Barber was sent in to bat for Deal and slammed a liner to left. Whiteman came tearing in at race-horse speed, lunged forward, caught the ball and, being carried off his feet by the momentum, turned a complete somersault and came up with the sphere grasped firmly in his hands. It was a marvelous play, executed in a brilliant manner, and snuffed out the last ray of the Cubs' hopes for victory.

Wally Schang, Boston catcher, also had a splendid defensive and offensive Series, recalled in a letter to Clark of September 12, 1954:

> Well do I remember the 1918 World Series. . . . I hit .444 in that series. Was sure a great thrill. . . . the greatest play I made in that series was when I got Charley Pick at the plate in a 2 to 1 game.

After the final and winning game of the 1918 Series, Manager Ed Barrow of the new champions repaired to the famous Copley Square Hotel in Boston, where he was observed by correspondent Robert Maxwell, of *Reach's Guide:*

> He was alone and had every appearance of a tired businessman instead of a winning manager. . . . He did not wear his hat over one eye or swagger through the lobby like a real important person, but stood . . . as modest and unassuming as a guy about to slide out of the hotel without indulging in the formality of paying his bill.

Ed Barrow would be the last Boston baseball manager to win the double crown. Perhaps, had he been able to see ahead into the distant Red Sox future, he might have anticipated, and with personal pleasure, that his modest and unassuming presence in the Copley Plaza would be in the later characteristic spirit and mold of eventual owner Tom Yawkey, a gentleman to be famous for many sterling qualities, among them modesty and humility.

1918 WORLD SERIES EMBLEMS

As to the alleged broken promise on the World Series Emblems of 1918, it provoked a prolonged dispute and enduring efforts by Harry Hooper and the author to obtain a reversal of the decision, but to no avail. West Point graduate and then Commissioner of Baseball General William D. Eckert, in a letter of January 7, 1966, responded to the author's appeal (with substantiating letters from Harry Hooper, Sad Sam Jones and Carl Mays) for a reversal:

> Commissioner Frick has turned over correspondence to me relating to the 1918 Red Sox. Included in this were letters from you.
> I appreciate your sincere interest in the matter and admire your efforts to assist these men. I would certainly be happy, personally, if I could resolve the matter in their favor.
> I am sure you can appreciate the difficulties in thoroughly reviewing something that happened almost fifty years ago. It is difficult for me to understand how, if an injustice had been done, it would not have been corrected earlier. I have, however, obtained and looked at files containing letters of the National Commission at that time and have considered the material you submitted.
> I have not had an opportunity to study all of this thoroughly, but would not feel qualified to pass on the merits of these cases at this late date from the information I have.
>
> W. D. ECKERT
> Commissioner of Baseball

In way of background, before the start of the fourth Series game in 1918 at Boston, the Cubs and Red Sox instructed their representatives, Les Mann and Harry Hooper, respectively, to threaten a strike if the new rule that players would share in only 75 percent of the gate receipts (and prices were not raised for this wartime Series) was not set aside, or if the winning players were not guaranteed $1,500 each and the losers $1,000 each.

The three Commissioners, Ban Johnson, August Herrmann and John Heydler, made no concessions, and Hooper and Mann issued a statement that their players had agreed to play for the sake of the public and wounded soldiers who were there to see the game. The eventual winners' checks were for $890.00 each and for the Cubs, $535.00 each, reflecting contributions to war charities.

According to rumor, there was a special order placed in the files of the Commission to the effect that the 1918 Red Sox were never to receive their championship emblems. At any rate, a number of Red Sox keenly felt this denial, especially those who had not or would not be on another World Champion club. These included Sam Agnew, Jean Dubuc, Hack Miller, Dave Shean, Fred Thomas and George Whiteman. These players, if alive, would have been interested in the settlement of the 1972 player strike as an example of later day player-management problems and arbitration that contrasted to their plight.

THIRD PERIOD: FRAZEE'S RUINATION OF RED SOX, 1919-1923

1919 SEASON

The results and statistics of Boston's players appear to speak for themselves, but, as usual in professional sports, continuing or new and different policies, and their causes, frequently originated in the front offices. It may be a short time or even a long period before management influences manifest themselves on the playing fields, but they always appear. A new, ominous and disastrous trend in Red Sox baseball was forming during Frazee's tenure.

Dropping to sixth place, the team experienced the first Boston year since 1908 when games lost exceeded games won. Chicago won the pennant and then went on to be engulfed by the 1919 World Series scandal. The Red Sox were a distant 20½ games back, because the typical Boston all-around balance and strength was gone. The team placed sixth both in ERA and batting. However, they were still first in fielding; but fine fielding never won a pennant and never will.

Six of the team's members did well. Ruth was a League standout as a result of Manager Barrow's adopting shrewd Captain Harry Hooper's suggestion to use the Babe in the outfield when he wasn't pitching. In 111 games as an outfielder, supplemented by additional bat appearances as a pitcher and first baseman, the Babe led the League in RBI, home runs (29, a new record), total bases and runs and was second in walks (101), positively indicating his general recognition as a very dangerous hitter. Not until Jimmie Foxx's arrival in 1936 would another Red Sox receive over 100 walks. Ruth was also 9-5 in his pitching. Herb Pennock's brilliant 16-8 was an isolated bit of brightness on the mound, in view of the fact that the club would not have an effective mound corps again until 1938. Veterans Schang and McInnis hit .306 and .305, respectively.

Sad Sam Jones slumped to 12-20, and Joe Bush was able to pitch only nine innings. A disgruntled Carl Mays, who had great difficulty in getting along with his teammates, allowed his dissatisfaction to get so far out of hand as to quit the team, and, when several clubs bid for his services, Frazee selected Ruppert's Yankees as the recipient. At the time, not too many people around Boston realized that the very wealthy Ruppert would be showing a steadily increasing interest in Red Sox players and would have very favorable situations in which to further his objectives.

TWO OUTSTANDING BABE RUTH STORIES

Both then and now, occasional manager-team captain confrontations occur. Back in this early period of American professional baseball, the selected team captain usually got an extra thousand dollars, as did Hooper, for his very valuable services, judgments and orders. In a detailed letter to Clark, Harry very kindly provided fascinating insights into "command" relations between Manager Barrow and himself and recalled a confrontation between Babe Ruth and Barrow, both incidents from the 1919 Boston season:

Ed was a strict disciplinarian, but he did not know baseball as a player does. . . . But he was smart enough to realize his own shortcomings as a manager. And I ran the club on the field. Only one time did we have words. I gave a sign to Al Walters [Red Sox catcher] to not give a good ball to a batter with two men in scoring position. My sign was to try to make him hit a bad ball. . . . the pitcher grooved one and the batter hit it and scored both runs. After the inning when I came in I was mad and was going to jump on Walters and find out why

FOURTEEN OF THESE MEN LIVED TO BE OVER 80! The 1911 Red Sox, with the then familiar Bull Durham sign in the background, posed for this picture little realizing their eventual achievements. Longevity leaders were: Nagle, 91, Gardner, 89, Lewis, 89, McHale, 88, Hooper, 87, Wood, 87, Riggert, 86, Gunning, 86, Carrigan, 85, Baker, 85, Cicotte, 84, Collins, 82, Yerkes, 82, Killilay, 81. This was the last team photo taken at Huntington Avenue. In 1976, the memory of these men was honored at Northeastern University, Boston. (*Courtesy of John Hooper*)

Articles of Agreement. between the *Boston American League Base Ball Club*

of the City of *Boston* , in the State of *Mass* a club member of a League known as the "American League of Professional Base Ball Clubs," party of the first part, and

Harry B. Hooper of the City of

Sacramento in the State of *Cal* , party of the second part,

Witnesseth:

1. That in consideration of the faithful performance, by the party of the second part, of the conditions, covenants, undertakings and promises hereinafter set forth, including the option in first party to terminate this contract, the said party of the first part agrees to pay unto second party the sum of *2850* per season, payable as follows: In semi-monthly installments on the first and fifteenth of each month during the period covered by this contract; unless this contract shall be terminated by the first party while the second party be "abroad" with the ball club of the first party for the purpose of playing games, in which event the installment then falling due shall be paid on the first week day after the return "home" of the ball club.

2. Said party of the second part agrees to perform for party of first part, and for no other party during the period of this contract (unless with the consent of said first party) such duties pertaining to the exhibition of the game of base ball as may be required of him by said party of the first part, at such reasonable times and places as said party of the first part may designate, for the American League season for the year 190_, beginning on or about the _____ day of _____ 1909, and ending on or about the _____ day of October, 190_, which period of time shall constitute the life of this contract, unless sooner terminated in accordance with the further provisions of this contract.

3. Party of the first part may, from time to time, during the continuance of this contract, establish reasonable rules for the government of its players "at home" and "abroad" and such rules shall be a part of this contract as fully as if herein written, and binding upon second party hereto; and for violation of these rules and for any conduct impairing the faithful and thorough discharge of the duties incumbent upon second party, may impose reasonable fines upon second party and deduct the amount thereof from any money due, or to become due, to second party herein.

4. It is further agreed that should second party be disabled or his ability to perform his duties be impaired at any time during the term herein prescribed, the said party of the first part may deduct from the amount then due or to become due under this contract, such proportion thereof as the period of said disability or impairment may bear to the term herein prescribed; but no such deduction shall be made by reason of any accident or injury received by second party while in performance of his regular duties under the direction of first party, unless such injury or accident shall wholly or partly incapacitate second party for a period of fifteen days, in which event this contract may be terminated at the option of first party.

5. It is further agreed, should party of the second part become disabled, as provided in the preceding section, that he will submit himself to medical examination and treatment by a regular physician, in good standing, to be selected by the first party, and such examination when made at the request of first party, shall be at the expense of said first party, unless made necessary by some act or conduct of second party contrary to the terms of this agreement or rules and regulations made under it.

6. It is further understood and agreed, that the said party of the first part shall furnish the said party of the second part with two complete uniforms, exclusive of shoes, for which the said party of the first part shall be allowed the sum of $30 toward the cost thereof, to be deducted from the wages or salary herein prescribed. And the said party of the first part shall provide and furnish the said party of the second part, while "abroad" or traveling with the "nine" or team in other cities, with proper board, lodging, and pay all proper and necessary traveling expenses.

7. In order to enable the party of the second part to fit himself for the duties necessary under the terms of this contract, the said party of the first part may require the said party of the second part to report for practice at such place as the party of the first part may designate and participate in such exhibition contests as may be arranged by said party of the first part for a period of *30* days prior to the _____ day of _____ the party of the first part to pay the actual hotel and traveling expenses of the said party of the second part, from the city of *San Francisco* during said period. In event of the failure of the party of the second part to report for practice a penalty of at least one hundred dollars may be imposed by party of the first part, same to be deducted from the compensation stipulated in this contract.

8. It is further understood and agreed, that the party of the first part may, at any time after the beginning and prior to the completion of the period of this contract, give the party of the second part ten days written notice to end and determine all its liabilities and obligations under this contract, in which event all liabilities and obligations undertaken by said party of the first part, in this contract, shall at once cease and determine at the expiration of said ten days; the said party of the second part shall thereupon be also freed and discharged from compensation. If such notice be given to the party of the second part while "abroad" with the club, he shall be entitled to his necessary traveling expenses to the city of *San Francisco*.

9. It is further understood and agreed between both parties to this contract that they will respect and abide by the Constitution, rules and edicts of said League, subject only to an appeal for final adjudication to the National Commission, and also respect and abide by all of the provisions and conditions of the National Agreement.

In Witness Whereof. The said party of the first part hath hereunto caused its common seal to be affixed and these presents to be subscribed by the president of said club, and the said party of the second part has hereunto set his hand and seal this *15th* day of *January* A. D. 1909.

John I. Taylor , President.

Boston Am. League Base Ball Club

Harry B. Hooper , Player.

SEAL

SEAL

WITNESSES PRESENT:

FOR LOVE OR MONEY? As Hooper would remark many times after 1909, he and the players of his vintage played more for love of the game and for the fun of competition than they did for the monetary gains. Salaries, as this contract indicated, were measured and restricted within a few thousand dollars, and if a player was fortunate enough to be selected captain of the team, an extra thousand dollars would be his. From the owners' points of view, baseball franchises were not gilt-edged investments; rather, they were to be regarded as quite precarious and mostly rewarding as an outlet for their own baseball interest and enthusiasm. Income was produced chiefly by gate receipts, with most admissions at less than a dollar, and a few ads in scorecards of very modest size. (*Courtesy of John Hooper*)

Jan 19th 1909.

Dear Hooper —

Enclosed find contract for 1909. at $2850. Will agree to pay transportation both ways but cannot put it in contract under the league rules. You can keep this letter for guarantee of that part.

Sign and return one contract to me, keeping the other. Will let you know what time to report at Hot Springs.

Yours sincerely,

John I. Taylor.

JOHN I. TAYLOR, CLUB PRESIDENT, 1904-1911. Taylor was both a remarkable and controversial man. He was dedicated, had a keen eye for baseball talent (as his signing of Hooper and Lewis amply proved), and made the very judicious selection of Red Sox for the team's nickname. He could and did write an effective business letter, of which this one is a typical example. Hooper was one of his favorites; on occasion he would buy him a new suit in recognition of his fine play or point to him with pride while telling intimates at the ball game that Harry was one of the boys. On the other hand, President Taylor had a short fuse when irritated or when adversity descended upon his team. (*Courtesy of John Hooper*)

Santa Cruz - 4-8-74

Dear Ellery,

I received your letter this morning. I will answer your questions in order as written -

But first about your essay on the greatest Red Sox Player ever's - It is hard to compare players except at the position they played. I played right all my career. I played some games in C.F. my first year in left field. but I played probably 95% of my games in right.

I played my first year in left field. Started in right but couldn't handle the sun. ~~Finally~~ Most right field parks have the sun in right. But while I played in left in 1909 - I practiced playing the sun field until I was good at it.

In 1910 - Duffy Lewis came up - they wanted more right handed hitters in the lineup. But Duffy couldn't play the sun field. So they shifted me to right and put Duffy in left. He broke up the first game he played, after we had lost several games to left handed pitchers before they made the switch. And from ~~that~~ day he never played any field except left. That was the beginning of the Outfield of Lewis - Speaker & Hooper in order left - Center & right.

PRACTICE IS THE NAME OF THE GAME. With typical Hooper foresight and determination, Harry taught himself how to play the difficult sunfield—right field—and set the stage for the greatest defensive outfield in both Boston and major-league baseball history. Later acknowledged to be peerless in his fielding sector, Hooper for years was obviously a great favorite of the old Boston right field bleacher-pavilion crowd, who delighted at his sliding and running catches as well as his hard, accurate throws that cut down advancing base runners.

February 1976

The outfield of Hooper, Speaker and Lewis was pretty good according to a number of people. Tres Speaker was the king of the outfield. If a player hit mostly to left field he would move Hooper over from right. It was the same moving around in every player. It was always take it or I got it. In all the years we never bumped each other. We all had good arms, and Ty Cobb knew it. Many a time he tried to make a double on a single but we got him many times. About the cliff "Duffy's" I used to go out and practice in the morning. You have to take one look at the ball. Or up if you have a chance to get it. You can't keep looking at the ball if you do down you go went you hit the bank. "Duffy's Cliff". In my day we did not have to look at third base to see what to do. We did every thing by our selves. Bat on hit an run. double steal and squeeze play.

GOOD COMMUNICATION ALSO THE NAME OF THE GAME. Lewis's letter should be read by every contemporary and prospective outfielder. The Red Sox outfield of Hooper-Speaker-Lewis, 1910-1915, never bumped in fielding confusion. Sound, quick decisions and brief commands or statements, as indicated, achieved this mastery of fluid fielding. In six years together, Hooper-Speaker-Lewis made exactly 455 assists, a record that will last forever and one that will enshrine them as the American League's greatest defensive outfield.

January 5, 1976

Dear Ellery! The Huntington Ave grounds was a small ball park. If you hit a home run you were doing something. In 1910 Jake Stahl hit ten homeruns to lead the league and I was second hitting eight. This was in some book that I read —

We used to go out in the morning to take batting practice a number of games in those days were 2 to 1 or 1–0. We were hitting against spit ball pitches. Today is diffent they have the lively ball to hit.

I remember in those days 1910 if we were behind some one on the bench would throw out a clean ball and if we were in front they would throw out a black ball — for the other club to hit

A number of players lived at Putnams Hotel. My first salary was 400 a month with transport to California "Duffy"

I was born fifty years to soon.

No air condition in those days on Railroads or Hotels.

HOME TEAM ADVANTAGE! As statistics prove, teams do better at home than away, for a variety of reasons. Not too many years ago, allegations were made that the Chicago White Sox were freezing baseballs hours before game time in order to limit the distances opposing batters might hit the ball. Another club was accused of over-watering their infield so as to reduce the speed of opposing batters. As indicated, back in 1910, if and when the home-standing Red Sox tossed in a new ball late in a game when they were batting, shrewd observers would realize that they needed runs. But should the Red Sox be in the field in the final innings, they would do their best to keep a discolored ball in play— "our boys" were ahead and doing their best not to give the visitors any batting advantages.

January 8, 1974

Dear Ellery: In my memory Duffy's
Cliff was about six or seven feet.
I can't recall the length.
The most thrilling game was the
Joe Wood - Walter Johnson game - Each
pitcher won sixteen straight. Speaker
doubled and I doubled. We won one 1 to 0
Another good one was in the 1915
series - Five hits off Grover Cleveland
Alexander in eight times at bat.
In the 1915 series I won two games
beating Alexander 2-1 and George Chalmers
2-1 and the last game of the series
I hit a home run off E. J. Ryley
One man on and two runs behind.
It was four to two. Tied up the game
and Hooper next inning hit a home
run winning the game - 5 to 4
The best catch I believe was in 1915
series off C. Cravath. Up the cliff.

KEEN MEMORIES AT AGE 85! The still very lively Duffy Lewis provided the author with a variety of most interesting information on aspects of his distinguished baseball career in a few well-selected words. The Matterhorn is officially listed as 14,690 feet, as mountain climbers well know. "Duffy's Cliff," which was a sharp incline of several feet in height, existed in Fenway Park from the construction of the field until Mr. Yawkey had the park rebuilt after the 1933 season. Duffy was a master at playing it; many others, both visitors and some latter-day Red Sox, were not.

HOW THE CATCH WAS ACTUALLY MADE! On January 27, 1974, Harry Hooper, at the author's request, for the first and only time in his life, sketched how the World Series-saving catch of 1912 was made. Over the years, many famous Boston baseball cartoonists have inaccurately depicted how the catch was made—thus the author's determination to get the record set straight by the one man who knew. On September 8, 1975, some months after Harry's passing, Harry Hooper, Jr., was kind enough to write: "Your account of the Great Moment involving Dad and Larry Doyle was simply he had not followed my sign. Before I could say anything Barrow asked what was the idea of giving the hitter a good ball to hit with an open base. Walters said, 'Hooper gave me the sign.' 'Hooper gave you the sign?' said Barrow. 'Since when has Hooper been managing the club?' I was mad and did not ask Walters why he called for a good pitch, whether he did or whether the pitcher did not intend to give him a good one. But I was mad and I said, 'O.K. And from now on you can run the club. I will play my position.'

I was the last one dressed. Ed was at the door. He said, 'Don't pay any attention to what went on on the bench. Just keep on the way you have been.' We never had any more words.

He [Barrow] had guts. Made Babe back down. He gave Babe a going over for being late to a meeting. Ruth said, 'You talk to me like that and I'll punch you in the nose.' Ed glared at him. 'You big ——————, I'll kill you.' He then went on with the meeting. When it was over he said, 'Ruth, you stay here.' Ruth was the first one out the door. We used to call Ed 'Simon Legree'.

In a 1970 letter to Clark, Hooper reviewed the background of Babe Ruth's becoming an outfielder for Boston in 1919:

Everett Scott, Heinie Wagner and I went to Ed Barrow and suggested putting Babe in the outfield. Nothing doing, said Ed. Why I would be the laughing stock of the League if I put the best left handed pitcher in the League in the outfield. In the meantime Ruth was hitting long balls while pitching. Barrow told us he had $50,000 invested in the club. One day I said to Ed, You have big money in the club. You are interested in hearing the turnstiles click. Have you noticed we have a larger crowd when Ruth pitches? Sure he answered. Ed I said—the crowds are coming out to see him hit. Why don't you put him in the outfield where he will be in the lineup every day? He saw the point and finally said, O.K. We'll put him in the outfield. But mark my word the first big slump he gets in he will be back on his knees begging me to pitch. So I put him in right field. We had another wild man in left, Roth. When a ball was hit to center I would holler for it but I could hear Ruth and Roth heading towards me. After a couple days I told Ed, I am going to put Ruth in center before I get killed out there and I went back to right field. Only had to be careful on one side. But Ruth was a natural and good outfielder from the start.

Another way to discern changing patterns and trends of a team is by noting the aura of the clubhouse atmosphere and conversation, which ordinarily is the opportunity of only the insiders, sometimes including well-liked, reliable reporters. Gradually, the generally happy, confident atmosphere and conversations of the Red Sox clubhouse changed, and, for various reasons, the high peak of such pleasant situations, as in 1915 and 1916, never again would be attained. Journeyman ball players, including many who were thought to be near the end of their careers or had not produced as well as their managers had expected, soon drifted into Fenway Park, often in exchange for Boston athletes still in their prime years or just approaching them. As the author well remembers, the Red Sox of the 1920s were a team of few words, and there was little cause for club happiness and expressions of it as they languished in the doldrums, awaiting a friendly and assisting breeze, if not a prevailing wind of hope. It would be delayed for some 16 years.

With the sale of Mays, the prelude to the great tragedy began. The first act occurred in January, 1920, when Ruppert proudly announced the purchase of Babe Ruth for $100,000. Unannounced was Ruppert's granting of a $350,000 mortgage on Fenway to Frazee. By 1922, Harry had wrecked the franchise. Schang, Hoyt, Bush, Jones, Scott, Pennock and Pipgras followed Mays and Ruth to New York and were integral factors in the rise and dominance of the Yankees who would win 6 pennants in the period 1921-1928. What did the above-mentioned players do for their new owners, and how did they complement the fearsome batting power that other players would inevitably provide the New Yorkers? In regular season play, Ruth eventually hit 659 home runs for them, while the combined records of Mays, Hoyt, Bush, Jones, Pennock and Pipgras would read 618-383 for a percentage of .617.

HARRY FRAZEE

Timing in life, more often coincidental than planned, is a determining factor in important events that may be detrimental or beneficial, dependent upon the point of view. This general statement is most applicable to Harry Frazee, Red Sox owner from late 1916 until the summer of 1923, and to those upon whom he cast his varying influences.

Frazee, when he bought the club, did so with insufficient money to support both his continuing and risky theatrical productions and the debts incurred by his baseball franchise purchase. Thus his initially precarious financial position worsened when a number of his stage enterprises did not do well in the critical period 1919 through 1922, resulting in his having to rob Peter to pay Paul.

Peter easily can be identified as a composite of his star Red Sox players and the dismayed Boston fans. Paul was a more complex symbol of many persons and differing interests. Ruppert had the leverage of his Fenway mortgage to assist him in lifting desired ball players to New York. He was quick on the draw of his check book to obtain desirable pounds of Red Sox baseball flesh in return for desperately needed Frazee money, which, in turn, promptly went on to his eager creditors, including those holding unpaid theatrical debts.

In the summer of 1923, Frazee sold the franchise to Bob Quinn, but the full irony of the Frazee-blighted years was yet to develop. Financial success was about to descend on Harry, no longer the owner. Opening in Chicago in 1924 and soon becoming a national and international success, his show, *No, No, Nanette,* would net him more than two million dollars. Additional irony was apparent to perceptive Red Sox fans who attended performances of this musical comedy. Its musical success was largely attributable to the public's warm reaction to Vincent Youman's three brilliant songs, including the title song and "Tea for Two."

But the most poignant of the three to Boston fans was, "I Want to Be Happy," with whose philosophy they could not have agreed more. Ex-owner Frazee might smile all the way to the bank, but Boston's faithful would continue to catalog him as their villain of baseball until his death and beyond.

William Shakespeare's well-known observations about all life being a stage and the sad interpretations of his remarks in Boston are forever associated with Harry Frazee and the contemporary twin masks of sorrow that both his theatrical and baseball enterprises wore in the depressed early years of 1920 through to the end of his Red Sox ownership.

FOURTH PERIOD:
1923-1933—
BOB QUINN'S PRESIDENCY
A DECADE OF DESPAIR

ON THE FIELD

For those who believe in the pendulum theory of history and in the applicability of this theory to the rise and fall of certain ball clubs, then chartists and theorists could have an impressive opportunity to compare and contrast the golden age of Red Sox baseball, a brief but marvelous 7 years, with the 15 discouraging ones that followed. From 1922 through 1932, the team would never get closer to .500 than minus 20 in 1924, and as far as minus 68 in 1932, and would finish last 9 years, never in the first division, and with an overall record of 752-1241 for a percentage of .377. If misery loves company, though not necessarily in the same exact time span, the record of the Philadelphia Athletics, limping in last in the 7 successive seasons 1915-1921, was even more depressing: 323-710 for an average of .312!

One of the most interesting conclusions, using statistics to establish certain trends and patterns of Red Sox baseball in this period, effectively can be presented in the following table and will save hundreds of words:

Commentary on Table 12: Quite obviously, comparing Red Sox batters and pitchers of these years with their opponents, the hitters were very weak, last for 11 consecutive seasons. Note the home run comparisons as an indication of Boston's lack of power; even the alibi that the old distances to right and center were greater does not excuse such offensive feebleness. Clearly, relatively few Bostons were even getting on base. On the other

Table 12

Year	Boston Finish	ERA Position	Batting Position	Team Points Behind Team Batting Leader	Boston Homers	Average League Team Homers
1920	5	4	7	39	22	44
1921	5	4	6	39	17	59
1922	8	6	8	50	45	65
1923	8	8	8	40	34	55
1924	7	4	8	21	30	49
1925	8	8	8	41	41	66
1926	8	8	8	36	32	53
1927	8	7	8	48	28	54
1928	8	7	8	32	38	60
1929	8	7	8	32	28	74
1930	8	3	8	45	47	84
1931	6	5	8	35	37	72
1932	8	8	8	39	53	88
Average	7	6	8	38	34	63

hand, the Red Sox pitchers were more impressive, in 9 of these years being better positioned in their respective categories than their hitters. In that lively ball period of baseball, lack of Boston RBI power negated the contributions of pitching that was below average but yet not too bad. 1930 is a very interesting season to consider as one example.

Boston finished last for the sixth consecutive year, at 52-102; yet in team ERA, they ranked behind only the first division teams. But because their run production was the worst in the league, 612, exactly 117 fewer than the seventh-place club, their pitchers did not get adequate offensive support. Thus, they did not have a single regular pitcher at or above .500, despite some good ERAs: Milt Gaston, 3.92, Dan MacFayden, 4.21, Hod Lisenbee, 4.40. What were their won-lost records? Gaston, 13-20, MacFayden, 11-14, and Lisenbee 10-17. In contrast, George Earnshaw, with good hitters behind him, won 22, lost 13, and had an ERA of 4.44 with the Philadelphia Athletics.

Freely admitting the unfairness of judging pitchers just by won-lost figures but using such records in the following table to indicate the remarkable achievement of weakly supported Boston pitching, I give special credit to these Boston individuals in the 1920-1932 period, all of whom labored uphill in effect.

Table 13

Year	Pitcher	Won	Lost	Notable League Achievement
1920	Pennock	16	13	
1921	Jones	23	16	First in League Shutouts, fourth in Wins, fifth in ERA
1921	Bush	16	9	Third in League Winning Percentage
1922	R. Collins	14	11	
1923	Ehmke	20	17	No-hitter against Philadelphia, second in League Innings and Complete Games, third in Wins, fourth in Strikeouts
1923	Quinn	13	17	Second in Saves
1924	Ehmke	19	17	First in Innings Pitched, second in Complete Games and Strikeouts, fifth in Wins
1924	Quinn	12	13	Third in Saves
1925	Ehmke	9	20	First in Complete Games, third in Strikeouts
1928	Morris	19	15	Third in Games Pitched, fifth in Saves
1928	Ruffing	10	25	First in Complete Games, second in Innings, fourth in Strikeouts
1929	MacFayden	10	18	Tied for first in Shutouts
1929	Ruffing	9	22	Fifth in Strikeouts
1931	Moore	11	13	First in Saves, second in Games Pitched
1931	MacFayden	16	12	

Ehmke was philosophical about his near-achievement of two successive no-hitters on the road in 1923. The breaks evened up. At Philadelphia, pitcher Slim Harriss seemingly had a double but failed to touch first, and it was noticed by both the umpire and Boston first baseman Joe Harris, and Ehmke's no-hitter was preserved. But in Howard's next appearance at Yankee Stadium, official scorer Fred Lieb as usual called them as he saw them and awarded Whitey Witt a hit on a controversial fielding play at third by Howard Shanks. That was the only Yankee safety of the game. To this day, he is the only Red Sox pitcher to win 20 games for a last-place club. As noted above, in his three full Boston seasons he was a standout, and Connie Mack was delighted to get him in 1926. Mack was even more pleased in the 1929 World Series when their mutually planned and surprise strategy of starting Howard against the Chicago Cubs resulted in a victory and Ehmke's making a new Series record for strikeouts, 13, in one game.

Five months earlier, on April 5, 1923, a friendship began that lasted until Howard Ehmke's passing in a Philadelphia hospital from a brain infection on March 17, 1959. He was to be like an older brother to the author for over 35 years.

Ehmke to Clark, April 5, 1923:

Your letter was received a few days ago and this is my first chance I have had to answer same. I always like to hear from young boys and make it a business to answer every letter. As far as autographing a baseball for you it would give me pleasure to do so. If you will please come to me sometime when you are out at Fenway ball park I will give you an autographed American League ball and the autographs you asked for. Please don't be afraid as I will be glad to meet you.

Thank you for wishing me so much success and **I am only** hoping I can come up to your expectations.

TRAGEDY OF ED MORRIS

"Big Ed" Morris started his brief (1928-1931) Red Sox career with an outstanding 19-15 for a hopeless team finishing 43½ games behind, and his eventual tragedy it was to be stabbed to death in March, 1932, during a Florida fish-fry just before his scheduled departure for the Boston training camp at Savannah. Earlier, he was the victim of an amusement-incurred accident, which began his pitching decline.

During the season, what a player does with his spare time has an important bearing on how he performs on the field. When a club is on the road, obviosuly the manager and his trusted lieutenants can and do keep a watchful eye on all this in the hotel of their use. What the individual players do for personal amusement, how they observe the curfews, what their liquor consumption, if any, may be, is a matter of concern to those charged with directing and leading the team.

In St. Louis, at the well-known baseball teams' hotel, the visiting Red Sox were guests, and Morris, bored with the quiet life of sitting on chairs, eating and sleeping, decided some close-at-hand diversion could be his. Dislodging the appointed elevator boy from his station, Ed temporarily captured and commandeered one of the elevators to the rising discontent of various house guests. Watching the up-down progress, the guests were in a rage at his not stopping to open the door. Management arrived and when unwary Ed finally opened the door at ground level, he was grabbed and a scuffle resulted, during which his pitching arm was severely twisted. Such an odd incident as this began the downfall of a very talented Boston player.

Red Ruffing deserves special comment. From 1925 until he went to the Yankees early in the 1930 season, his Red Sox record was 39-96. But this deceived nobody, especially the Yankees, who noticed very quickly his consistent strength and strikeout ability. Leaving behind a weak Boston batting attack, which had been .266, .256, .259, .264 and .267 for his full Red Sox seasons, he was supported by robust team averages of .309, .297, .286, .283, and .278 in his first five New York years. In 14 campaigns for the Yankees, he had a consecutive streak of four 20-game seasons (1936-1939) and compiled an overall record of 216-118.

EHMKE SAID IT WASN'T TRUE

From time to time, fans and sometimes even management claim in the case of obviously good pitchers and other players toiling for a hopeless club, that ball players are not putting out their utmost, for two reasons. One, it isn't worth it, and two, their lethargy may help their trade or sale to a contender. Boston fans claimed this was true, both of Ruffing and Ehmke. The author, then as later a privileged person to Ehmke's emotions and opinions, clearly remembers how upset Howard was, not long before his trade to the Athletics, when it was reported to him that Bob Quinn had accused him of not doing his best. How astonished he was to hear these words. Howard's shoulder was not good and had been subject to treatment at Battle Creek. As the author long knew Ehmke, he is convinced that he did not slacken his efforts for the Red Sox, and being a sensitive person, as had been shown in his earlier unhappy days at Detroit under the direction of the driver Ty Cobb, he was disturbed at Quinn's conversation. A person of tougher emotional fiber would have shrugged it off, but not Howard.

RED SOX INDIVIDUAL BATTING: 1920-1932

Year	Name	Batting Average	Notable League Achievement
1920	Tim Hendryx	.328	
	Harry Hooper	.312	Third in Triples and Walks
	Wally Schang	.305	
	Mike Menosky	.297	Fourth in Stolen Bases
1921	Derrill Pratt	.324	
	Stuffy McInnis	.307	
	Nemo Leibold	.306	
	Mike Menosky	.300	
1922	Joe Harris	.316	
	George Tioga Burns	.306	
	Derrill Pratt	.301	Second in Doubles
1923	Joe Harris	.335	
	George Tioga Burns	.328	Second in Doubles
	Ira Flagstead	.312	
1924	Ike Boone	.333	Fifth in Home Runs
	Ira Flagstead	.305	
	Joe Harris	.302	
	Bill Wambsganss	.274	Third in Doubles
1925	Ike Boone	.330	
	Roy Carlyle	.326	
	Doc Prothro	.313	
	Ernie Vache	.313	
1926	Bill Jacobson	.305	
	Emory Rigney	.270	Third in Walks
1927	John Tobin	.310	
1929	Buddy Myer	.313	First in Stolen Bases
	Ken Williams	.303	
	John Rothrock	.300	Fourth in Stolen Bases
	Russ Scarritt	.294	Second in Triples
1930	Earl Webb	.323	
1931	Earl Webb	.333	First in Doubles, 67, a new and still existing major league record
1932	Dale Alexander	.367	Red Sox' first batting champion. Actually hit .372 for Boston after coming from Detroit
	Roy Johnson	.299	Third in Stolen Bases

Commentary: In general, these above average hitters were passing through the ever-changing baseball scene, particularly so when a club is a steady loser, and averaged just under 2½ years with the Red Sox, by coincidence similar to that of their unsmiling managers. Jack Rothrock, seven years, Ira Flagstead, six, Roy Johnson and Mike Menosky, four each, were the longest associated, and these tenures were indications of their value to Boston.

1920-1930 RED SOX LEAGUE-LEADING FIELDERS

Stuffy McInnis, first baseman, topped the League in both 1920 and 1921 with first a .996 rating, and in 1921 a new major league mark of .999. Shortstop Everett Scott, ending his Boston service, stretched his record as League fielding champion to six straight by leading both years, with .973 and .972, respectively. The team was best in 1920 and 1921 League fielding. Later Red Sox shortstops Emory Rigney in 1926, and Hal Rhyne, in 1931, also prevailed. Successors to McInnis at first also were titlists: Phil Todt, in 1928, and Bill Sweeney, in 1931. Center fielders Ira Flagstead, in 1927, and Tom Oliver, in 1931, won fielding crowns, first since Amos Strunk's of 1918. But these fielding achievements were of little value to the depressed club.

FOURTH PERIOD: 1923-1933— BOB QUINN A VICTIM OF CIRCUMSTANCES

IN THE FRONT OFFICE

For a second time in the twentieth century, money became a big factor in the possible rise or continued struggle of the Red Sox. Whereas Frazee had become the victim of his own financial entanglements and strangulations by which the team had been crushed, the new owner, Bob Quinn, recent Vice President of the St. Louis Browns, had high hopes and sincere intentions of putting the Bostons back in the race as soon as possible. The franchise was available for just over a million dollars in the summer of 1923, and Quinn, financially supported by wealthy Palmer Winslow, invested all his available money. But the harsh realities of the overall situation soon dissipated the dream, which became an impossible one. He was steadily assailed by numerous and mounting problems, of which money was the most serious.

Winslow's health collapsed and months later he died, cutting off the monetary help upon which Quinn had depended. In the ten years of his unhappy regime, Bob's ball team finished last eight times, once sixth and once seventh. Well beyond his control was the Great Depression and its American manifestations. Additionally, local Boston weather conditions produced rain on many critical at-home dates when the club was trying hard and potential crowds were eager to support them. Paid attendances of course reflected these serious adversities; four seasons were under 300,000 and another four between 300,000 and 400,000.

On the player front, Quinn had no luck in discovering potential long-career star players, and the lack of an effective farm system hurt. Most of the players acquired either were rookies who did not make it, or veterans who were considered either washed up or expendable problems by their managers. A few, such as Howard Ehmke and Ira Flagstead, produced excellently. Ruppert was still buying and he had a keen ear for Quinn's financial problems. Red Ruffing and Dan MacFayden were sold at bargain prices, especially in reflective view of Ruffing's forthcoming sustained prominence for the New Yorkers.

As the months passed, it became increasingly obvious to Bob that he could not make his desires come true, especially since he was burdened with debts amounting to over a third of a million and no prospects of financial improvement. Thus, in the spring of 1933, when Thomas A. Yawkey came into his vast inheritance and had a great ambition to own a major league ball club, Quinn had his opportunity to get out. Greatly disappointed by the cruel buffets that undeservedly had been his lot, he sold the club, honorably paid off his debts and was ready to continue life's unending battle again, rich only in experience, yet not crushed by the turn of events.

Thus ended the second great act in the drama of money affecting the Boston Red Sox. Soon the third act would bring smooth financial seas for the franchise and occasional pennants as Mr. Yawkey would create a record for Red Sox individual ownership—44 seasons—from the spring of 1933 into the summer of 1976.

In retrospect, there appears to have been a major lesson from acts one and two—the ownerships of Frazee and Quinn. Had they been men of independent wealth, there would have been a strong chance that the Boston team rather than the New York club would have dominated the League and that the then Boston stars or potential stars would have continued to wear the Red Sox uniform, such as Ted Williams, Bob Doerr, Dom DiMaggio, Tex Hughson, and Boo Ferriss would do in the service of Tom Yawkey.

As a then 14- and 15-year old, the author remembers with

mixed pleasure and sadness visiting Mr. Quinn on several occasions in his office at Fenway Park, at the suggestion of close friend Howard Ehmke who said, "Mr. Quinn would like to meet some Boston youngsters and talk about baseball, how they think the team will do and how boys' interest may be increased."

Mr. Quinn was always polite, inquiring and showed an ability to think and speak on boys' level when talking to them. The future author felt sad when things did not work out for Bob because he knew how dedicated and hopeful the owner was, and it seemed a great shame that a gentleman with his sincerity would be denied success for reasons well beyond his control. But that is a lesson of life hardest on the actual participant. Bob left Boston with many friends, including a considerable group from the then younger generation. What the author best remembers about him over these many years is not that he tried and lost but that he stood out as a fine, dedicated, sincere and religious man who had the best interests of the club and its fans at heart.

BOB QUINN'S MANAGERS

As Harry Hooper is quoted as saying elsewhere in this volume, in effect, you cannot win without the necessary horses or talent; proof of his truism was soon learned, if not before, when the parade of unhappy Red Sox managers began. After continuing Frank Chance, who had been Frazee's selection, through season 1923, wherein Frank's charges finished last, a sad contrast to his earlier playing on and managing four champion teams of the Chicago Cubs, Quinn brought in his friend Lee Fohl from the Browns. Lee had piloted the Indians and Browns to six consecutive years of second- or third-place finishes. For Boston, he was 7-8-8 in 1924-1926. Bill Carrigan, the peerless Red Sox leader of 1915-1916, was coaxed out of retirement for 1927-1929 and had basement teams each year. Next came a veteran Red Sox playing hero of 1906-1918, Heinie Wagner. One season was enough for him. Shano Collins, a Boston native who had been the regular Boston right fielder in 1921, also with considerable service in 1923 and 1924, took the helm in 1931, only to resign in mid-June the next season when he realized the team was on its way to a club record in futility, an eventual 111 defeats. Marty McManus, former Browns' and Tigers' infielder, had been acquired by the Red Sox late in the 1931 season and replaced Collins for the balance of 1932 and all of 1933. Marty, during his managerial service for Boston played the various infield positions, which momentarily may have eased his woes.

BIG-LEAGUE MANAGER—A PRECARIOUS POSITION

Quinn appointed five managers in his 10-year tenure. Theoretically, if they had been hired all at once, as a managership by committee, and assuming the best talents of each would have been used, there is no belief that the caliber of ball players they then had could have been improved materially. Whatever the professional sport may be, and assuming a poor position and weak prospects of a particular club, it seems a continuing marvel that candidates for managerships or coaches are rather plentiful. It may indicate a certain type of daring personality and personal philosophy that anticipates various stimulating returns from challenging the odds of prospective continued defeat. It is not believed that prospective managers include depressives, ones who enjoy defeat and gain satisfaction from this inversion of the ordinary attitude. Most prospective managers have to be natural-born optimists and must have great faith and confidence both in their own abilities and their skill in transplanting them into others. Many an ex-player has a burning, unquenchable desire to manage, despite the odds. A new manager may not have the talent or hopes of it, but to such gallant breeds this is not a deterrent. For the manager who beats such odds, triumphs are indeed wonderful. None of the Boston managers of this period were able to grasp the difficult success for which they had reached.

FIFTH PERIOD:
THE YAWKEY YEARS,
1933-1976—DEDICATION,
ENTHUSIASM, MONEY, PROBLEMS,
AND THREE PENNANTS

1933-1945

Dedication, enthusiasm and money were insufficient to produce an immediate or near-immediate pennant at Fenway Park, as the complexities of building a championship team soon became apparent. There was no quick miracle at Jersey Street, renamed Yawkey Way in 1977, but Mr. Yawkey's outstanding qualities would never weaken and time would be on his side. By the late 1930s and early and mid-1940s, the successful preludes to a 1946 pennant were accomplished: development of a farm and scouting system; growth of their own stars; temporarily coming out from the shadow of Yankee domination; a few timely, helpful trades; and a strong group-confidence of players returning from the armed services when World War II ended. Mr. Yawkey's baseball report card, 1934 through 1945, showed an A for effort and a B for achievement, with the team averaging fourth position in the group of 8 American League clubs.

Mr. Yawkey had to begin from behind the starting line in 1933, inheriting a team that in the year before was the worst in club history but would rise one notch that season. Acquiring ownership less than two months before the 1933 campaign began, obviously the new owner could not accomplish very much in player acquisitions. However, Yawkey began very logically and soundly, satisfying both sentimental and professional aims, by signing Eddie Collins, with Connie Mack's permission, as his baseball-wise Vice President and General Manager.

Collins, a great boyhood hero of Mr. Yawkey, had sterling credentials. A very prominent second baseman from 1906 through 1930, Eddie had a career mark of .333 and 9 times was the League's best fielder at his position. He was also a prolific base stealer in his prime for the Athletics and White Sox. In 1939, he would be chosen for Hall of Fame membership. In 1933, he was Connie Mack's right-hand man and coach, a dual role that soon would be very helpful to the Red Sox, as Collins's continuing friendship with Mr. Mack would aid in the purchase of many Philadelphia stars not necessarily over the baseball hill.

OUTSTANDING YAWKEY ACQUISITIONS

It is a fact that many players acquired by purchase or trade did not do too well for the Red Sox for various reasons; nevertheless, in the period 1933 through 1938, 8 acquired players contributed a great deal, and their "good" years at Boston almost equaled their "good" years for their previous American League teams:

Table 14

Name	Red Sox Period	"Good" Boston Years	"Good" Previous Years
Rick Ferrell	1933-1937	4	4 (St. Louis)
Lefty Grove	1934-1941	5	7 (Philadelphia)
Wes Ferrell	1934-1937	3	4 (Cleveland)
Joe Cronin	1935-1945	7	6 (Washington)
Jimmie Foxx	1936-1942	6	8 (Philadelphia)
Doc Cramer	1936-1940	5	4 (Philadelphia)
Joe Heving	1938-1940	3	2 (1 with Chicago 1 with Cleveland)
Lou Finney	1939-1945	5	6 (Philadelphia)
	Totals	38	41

These comparisons clearly show the soundness of Collins's earlier judgment on the future value to Boston of these experienced players. In particular, Foxx, Cronin and Grove would establish themselves in a number of Red Sox All-time Leaders' categories.

NEW FENWAY PARK, 1934

Mr. Yawkey simultaneously realized, from the fans' points of view, that both the setting and staffing of his rebuilding teams should be much more than merely adequate. He had the old park torn down and a new structure was built, to which he soon added the best available players in a twin effort to create, Phoenix-like from the metaphorical ashes of the old franchise, something of which to be proud. Opening Day, April 17, 1934, saw the new Fenway Park and its players making debuts, and although Washington beat them, in extra innings, Boston's faithful knew that the long corner of sustained adversity had been turned.

Four months later, on August 12, a doubleheader at home against the Yankees produced a record attendance at Fenway; 41,766 stuffed the park, and the author well recalls standing in deep left field, with Boston mounted police containing the standees, as a one-day ground rule was established, limiting to two bases a ball hit into the crowd. Mr. Yawkey, in the opinion of Boston fans, had arrived, and this tribute to him and his improved club would never be exceeded in the combination of enthusiasm, gratitude and total attendance.

Bucky Harris, though manager only for the one year 1934, had the personal distinction of leading the club to fourth place, the highest point of team attainment since the championship of 1918.

JOE CRONIN, 1935-1947

Yawkey and Collins after the 1934 season made headlines throughout the country's sports pages with the purchase, for a quarter of a million (a gigantic figure in those days), of Clark Griffith's son-in-law, Joe Cronin, who would both manage and play shortstop. Joe ultimately would manage for 13 years, 1935-1947, and bat his way into 8 categories of Red Sox' All-time Records:

Table 15

Category	Position	Achievement
Doubles	5	270
RBI	6	737
Slugging Percentage	5	.484
Extra Base Hits	7	433
Batting	10	.300
Games	10	1,134
Runs	10	645
Total Bases	10	1,883

MOE BERG, RED SOX' .261 HITTER, OVER .400 IN ERUDITION

From 1935 to the end of his major-league career in 1939, catcher Moe Berg, a distinguished Princeton graduate and previously with 4 other big-league clubs, graced the Red Sox with his fascinating presence. Much more in the bullpen than on the playing field (he averaged just under 30 games a season for Boston), Moe helped many players and aided one batboy to further his education.

Berg was better known for his off-field accomplishments, including his being much in demand at important dinners and other gatherings, and ultimately as a great patriot, as the biography discusses. He was a very individualistic dynamo of energy, ability, and friendship, and he possessed an insatiable thirst for as much knowledge as possible. His own development of language capabilities was exercised when he frequently gathered all the foreign newspapers available and used his marvelous fast-reading comprehension and retention skills.

The author remembers him one morning, when Boston was on a home stand, on the second floor of a then famous Scollay Square bookstore. Moe had created a physical situation comparable to the trench defenses of World War I's Western Front. Surrounded by stacks of scholarly books of his own piling, he was absorbing, with camera-eye ability, some specific scientific information when the author suddenly thrust a 1912 World Series program before him. Eagerly reaching up, Moe read it with amazing speed, then chuckled, as he handed it back, at the remark made therein to the American stage and George Arliss in comparison with the then champion Red Sox. It is sad that in Moe's last years, the buffets of life were to hit him and, in the opinion of his few intimates, made them far less enjoyable than he deserved.

As a result of Mr. Yawkey's 1934 through 1945 efforts, both the club's performance and the fans' approval were greatly improved, in comparison with the preceding years, 1921 through 1933:

Table 16
FENWAY PARK PAID ATTENDANCE, 1933-1945

Year	Position	Won	Lost	Attendance
1933	7	63	86	268,715
1934	4	76	76	610,640
1935	4	78	75	558,568
1936	6	74	80	626,895
1937	5	80	72	559,659
1938	2	89	62	646,459
1939	2	89	62	573,070
1940	4	82	72	716,234
1941	2	84	70	718,497
1942	2	93	59	730,340
1943	7	68	84	358,275
1944	4	77	77	506,975
1945	7	71	83	603,794

As indicated in the preceding table, the team had four second-place finishes, each time behind the outstanding Yankees. Boston was very good, New York better. Below, certain important selected stats show how these two fine clubs compared in certain respects and suggest significant reasons why they finished 1-2 each time:

Table 17

SELECTED COMPARISONS, RED SOX AND YANKEES

1938	Position	Won	Lost	Games Behind	ERA	Saves	Wins First Five Pitchers	Batting	HR	RBI by 6 Leading Regulars
New York	1	99	53	—	3.91	13	78	.274	174	637
Boston	2	88	61	9½	4.46	15	65	.299	98	621
1939										
New York	1	106	45	—	3.31	26	70	.287	166	606
Boston	2	89	62	17	4.56	20	56	.291	124	609
1941										
New York	1	101	53	—	3.53	26	63	.269	151	536
Boston	2	84	70	—	4.19	11	57	.283	124	572
1942										
New York	1	103	51	—	2.91	17	77	.269	108	508
Boston	2	93	59	9	3.44	17	64	.276	103	496

Commentary on Table 17: The Yankees consistently had better and more pitching depth. Johnny Murphy led the League in saves for these four years with a total of 56, only 7 less than the entire bullpen crew of the Red Sox. Ruffing, 71, Gomez, 45, Chandler, 40, and Donald, 33, were the big winners for the four years; Boston's best were Grove, 29, Wilson and Wagner, each 26, Ostermueller, 24, and Dobson, 23.

Although Boston team batting consistently was superior, the Yankees managed to drive in necessary runs and out-RBIed their closest rivals, 599 to 449. In home runs, the New Yorkers also prevailed, by the large margin of 599 to 449. As a group, Joe DiMaggio, Joe Gordon, Charley Keller, Tom Henrich, Bill Dickey and Red Rolfe appear to have had an edge over Ted Williams, Jimmie Foxx, Bob Doerr, Joe Cronin, Jim Tabor, and Joe Vosmik, but this is controversial. It is assumed that the will to win between the two clubs was about the same, although many assert the team leadership and general heroic image of Joe DiMaggio had much to do with the Yankee successes. He also batted in 505 runs and hit 113 homers in these four years as tangible assets.

JIMMIE FOXX

Jimmie Foxx (1936-1942), although with the Red Sox for only 7 years, as compared with Williams's 19, Yastrzemski's 16 to date, and Doerr's 14, hit his way into both club and League records, as follows:

able 18

AMERICAN LEAGUE SEASONAL ACHIEVEMENTS

Category	Position in Category (Number of Times)				
	1	2	3	4	5
Slugging Average	2		1		1
Home Runs	1	2	1	1	
Batting	1	1			
Total Bases	1	1		1	
RBI	1				
Walks	1				
Runs			1	1	
Hits			1		
Totals	**7**	**5**	**7**	**3**	**1**

Most Valuable Player, 1938

Table 19

BOSTON ALL-TIME CAREER BATTING

Category	Position	Record
Slugging Average	2	.605
Batting	3	.320
RBI	4	788
Home Runs	4	222
Extra Base Hits	6	448
Runs	7	721
Totals Bases	8	1,988

1946-1950: ONE SUCCESS, TWO FRUSTRATIONS, ONE CLOSE

Table 20

Year	Position	Won	Lost	Net Gain or Loss in Games over Previous Season	Team ERA	Team Batting
1945	7	71	83	− 6	8	2
1946	1	104	50	+33	4	1
1947	3	83	71	−21	6	2
1948	2	96	59	+12½	3	3
1949	2	96	58	+ ½	4	1
1950	3	94	60	− 2	6	1

In any renaissance, baseball or otherwise, the times must be right for change and improvement; there must be effective, dedicated people available to try to achieve the desired progress and others present to appreciate and support these efforts.

Anticipation of success is an important factor in gathering momentum, and Boo Ferriss has reviewed its influence:

Boo Ferriss to Clark, letter of January 28, 1977:

> I feel my 21-10 freshman season in 1945 was largely due to a Red Sox team that supported me well at bat and in the field although we finished in seventh place. It was a good feeling to know, however, that Williams, Doerr, DiMaggio and Pesky would be around in '46 and greatly improve our club.

The 1946 Red Sox met all the winning qualifications. World War II finally was over, and in their zealous postwar exuberance, the Boston fans would be behind the team to the point of exhilaration. Among the returning Red Sox, eager to swap armed services' uniforms for those of the Boston club, were Ted Williams, John Pesky, Dom DiMaggio, Tex Hughson, Joe Dobson, Mickey Harris and Hal Wagner. Boo Ferriss was a holdover from 1945, when he had been the ace with a 21-10 record. To round out the prospective all-around Red Sox power, two key players were obtained from Detroit—first baseman Rudy York and third baseman Mike Higgins. There was a team air of quiet confidence, as DiMaggio later wrote the author, "My memory of the 1946 season is one of pleasure throughout the entire year, with confidence very prevalent." Ferriss also emphasized the same point, and more:

Ferriss to Clark, January 28, 1977:

> In 1946 we put the pitching and hitting together as most everyone had a good season and we had a strong bench. We got off to a real good start, and quickly realized we had a real opportunity to go all the way and beat the Yankees and Tigers, our most serious challengers. There was good spirit on the club.

Unlike the very poor start the club would make in both 1948 and 1949, which had a great deal to do with their losing the pennant both times, the 1946 Bostons started like an atomic bomb. Almost invincible at home, they eventually won 60 of 77 games, to the cheers of a record-breaking season's total crowd of 1,427,315. On the road they were a creditable 44-33. Clinching the pennant on September 13 at Cleveland with the combination of Hughson's shutout and Williams's only career inside-the-park home run, the Boston team finally ended the season a dozen games ahead of Detroit, the dethroned champions.

On the importance of Manager Joe Cronin, Ted Williams wrote in his autobiography, *My Turn At Bat* (New York: Simon and Schuster, 1968):

> Cronin did a great job in 1946, when he managed from the bench. Cronin was a real ballplayer's manager and he was great to me. . . . There were so many things I loved about Joe Cronin. When he chewed me out I deserved it.
> . . . he was always stirring up the hitters, getting them talking, dragging information out of them. He had been a great player, he could do the things he talked about. . . . Cronin always made sure we got enough batting practice.

When the League's official season's statistics were compiled, the Boston club clearly had dominated. First in team batting and fielding and a creditable fourth in ERA, a Boston player appeared in almost every category of leaders:

Table 21

RED SOX PITCHERS, 1946

Name	Won	Lost	Special League Achievement
Ferriss	25	8	Third in Strikeouts and Innings, Fourth in Victories, Fifth in Winning Percentage and Complete Games
Hughson	20	11	First in Winning Percentage, Second in Games Pitched, Third in Complete Games and Innings
Harris	17	9	Fourth in Winning Percentage
Dobson	13	7	
Klinger	3	2	First in Individual Saves. Boston also led in total Team Saves

Table 22

RED SOX 1946 LEAGUE BATTING,
FIELDING AND SPECIAL AWARD ACHIEVEMENTS

Name	Batting Average	Special League Achievement
Williams	.342	American League's Most Valuable Player, First in Slugging Average, Total Bases, Runs and Walks. Second in Batting, RBI and Home Runs
Pesky	.335	First in Hits, Second in Runs, Third in Batting and Doubles
DiMaggio	.316	Fifth in Batting
York	.276	Third in RBI
Doerr	.271	Fourth in Batting, Second Base Fielding Leader .986

The club looked forward with anticipation to the World Series against the formidable St. Louis Cardinals, who had won a 2-game playoff against Brooklyn for the National League pennant. The Red Sox also had a 5-0 World Series record in back of them, contributed by the teams of 1903, 1912, 1915, 1916 and 1918, and Boston fans hoped the successful past would influence the present of 1946.

1946 WORLD SERIES

Baseball team won and lost records overwhelmingly prove it is less difficult to win at home than on the road, although the 1976 Yankees disproved this contention. Obviously, this is a factor in World Series play when more than four games have to be contested. Since the 1921 Series, the best of seven games has been the requirement. In even years, such as 1946, the National League champions have the home advantage, in odd years, the American League winners. This means playing the first two games at home, then the next three, if the Series goes that far, away, and, if a sixth and/or seventh game be necessary, back home again. In the final games of their earlier participation, the Red Sox had won the Series of 1903, 1912, 1916 and 1918 at home, and that of 1915 away.

The 1946 Series summaries are well known. In the opener at St. Louis, McBride's hit tied the game in the ninth and York's home run in the tenth won for Boston. In the second, Harry Brecheen, whose regular season 15-15 had been disarming, because he had been second in National League shutouts, fourth in wins and fifth in ERA, won his first of three games by besting Harris and Dobson, 3-0. Returning to Fenway, Ferriss blanked the visitors, 4-0, but the next day the Cardinals evened it up, with a 12-3 massacre against a parade of 6 Red Sox pitchers. Dobson put the Red Sox in the lead by winning 6-3 and the rivals entrained to St. Louis to settle matters.

Brecheen won a must game, 4-1, for his second triumph, and the next day, St. Louis won its second World Championship in five years, 4-3, with Brecheen, appearing in relief, staving off the Red Sox in the ninth. In the top of the eighth, Red Sox trailing, 3-1, Dom DiMaggio banged a double off the outfield wall to score both Russell and Metkovich, who had singled. But Dom pulled a leg muscle and had to leave the game immediately after reaching second base. The Cardinals in their half, with singler Enos Slaughter on and one out, pulled ahead on Walker's double, which replacement center fielder Leon Culberson probably played less effectively than an injury-free DiMaggio would have. Intelligent Slaughter, realizing that the odds were in his favor and that the surprise element also might be with him, without mental or physical pause kept on running and crossed the plate. Meanwhile, shortstop Pesky had taken the relay from Culberson and momentarily hesitated before making his throw toward his catcher. In the top of the ninth, although the Red Sox got two men on, Brecheen prevented any further scoring.

Individual Red Sox Series' performances varied. Williams was limited to 5 singles in 25 appearances, Hughson and Harris did not win a game between them, and their catchers made just one hit in 23 at bats. But Joe Dobson had an outstanding 0.00 ERA in his 12⅔ innings, Russell a useful 2 for 2 performance, and York won a game with one of his two homers. Moses's .417 and Doerr's .409 were achievements of which to be proud.

Yet, even though the team had lost, there probably was some enduring inspiration from the past and not from an earlier champion Boston team. As Bob Doerr wrote the author, March 2, 1955:

> There were several thrills I had while with the Red Sox. Going to spring training the first year [1937] and seeing such players as Foxx, Higgins, Cronin, Grove, the Ferrell brothers and others that I had read about then got to see and play alongside.

The memory of the seventh game was a long and enduring one, not yet ended. On February 16, 1970, Dom DiMaggio wrote the author:

> On the field of play, being in the 1946 World Series was tops and driving in the tying runs in the 7th game was equal, only to have to leave the game with a pulled leg muscle. We later lost that game and the World Series on Slaughter's famous run which turned out to be one of my greatest disappointments —because I was watching from the bench instead of participating in that particular play.

Boo Ferriss, 1-0 in the Series, also identified losing the Series as his greatest disappointment. But Bob Doerr, 21 years later as the first-base coach of the 1967 champion Red Sox, would realize the direct thrill and pleasure for a second time, but in the important coaching box rather than on the playing field.

Transportation on and off the field is always part of the game, whether you be a player or a traveling secretary. Slaughter's churning legs activated by Walker's hit had settled the Series. This event led to a St. Louis railroad station and the returning, defeated Red Sox team. In contrast to their happy, victorious predecessors, who traveled by train from New York after winning the League championship in 1904, and the World Champions of 1915, who traveled by rail from Philadelphia for Boston (both with sustained, bubbly conversations), the 1946 club had many unspoken thoughts and few words. No doubt, the earlier return trips of 1904 and 1915 had seemed fast and perhaps some even identified the hum of the wheels on the track as saying, "Red Sox! Red Sox!" But for the 1946 men, the journey home seemed almost endless, because of the intensification and protraction of sad emotions. Air flights materially reduce the immediate time-span of disconsolate thoughts and emotions, or their appreciated exuberant opposites.

The joys of 1946 were short-lived. As earlier in the late autumn of 1912, in the fall of 1946 visions of multiple pennants danced before the eyes of Red Sox enthusiasts. But the similarities ended at that point. Unlike the Red Sox of 1915, 1916 and 1918, the later editions of 1948 and 1949 each would miss by a single game and 1950's team would be as close as the original team of 1901, within 4 of the top. But there was one important similarity; the club of 1913 and that of 1947 would fail to repeat primarily because of crippling injuries, earlier, to pitcher Joe Wood, later in a triple exacta of arm injuries to three key hurlers —Ferriss, Hughson and Harris. In eight words, Dom DiMaggio summed it up to the author: "The 1947 season was disastrous because of injuries."

Ferriss summed up the adverse influences in a letter dated January 28, 1977:

> Arm injuries to Hughson, Harris and myself during the 1947 season dealt a serious blow to our winning again. The three of us, along with Joe Dobson, were being counted on to again do most of the pitching. This was certainly disheartening. I think the desire and spirit were there in '47 but these critical injuries to our pitching staff were more than we could overcome.

In contrast to 1946, the injuries torpedoed the heart of Red Sox pitching, with a net loss of 33 games that Joe Dobson, Denny Galehouse and Earl Johnson could not make up:

Table 23

Name	Won	Lost	Innings	Won	Lost	Innings
		—1946—			—1947—	
Ferriss	25	6	274	12	11	218⅓
Hughson	20	11	278	12	11	189⅓
Harris	17	9	222⅔	5	4	51⅔
Totals	62	26	774⅔	29	26	459⅓

Joe Dobson had a splendid year, at 18-8, and finished second in League winning percentage and fourth in wins. Earl Johnson, 12-11, placed third in games pitched and fifth in saves. Galehouse, 11-7, rounded out what remained of the pitchers.

On the offense, two members of the old guard came through handsomely. Williams, at .343, was in 9 League-leading categories: first in batting, RBI, home runs, slugging average, total bases, walks and runs; second in doubles; and third in hits. Pesky, .324, was first in runs, third in batting and stolen bases, fifth in total bases. York's 1946 RBI total of 119 was missed; after 27 more in early 1947, he went to the White Sox.

Following the 1947 disappointments, chiefly caused by pitching injuries, the fans, the team and Mr. Yawkey did not lose heart. Red Sox attendance in 1948 and 1949 set new records and although 1950's attendance was slightly lower, it would not be surpassed until pennant-year 1967. Mr. Yawkey began at the top, promoting Joe Cronin, after 14 years as manager, to General Manager and brought in 60-year-old Joe McCarthy, a 21-season pilot, first for the Cubs, later for the Yankees, who won 8 pennants, all but one with the New Yorkers. Interestingly, Joe McCarthy had no major-league playing background and proved very good managers do not necessarily have to be the products of the playing fields of major-league teams.

MORE THOUGHTS ON MANAGERS

The effect of the change of managership upon the Boston team was important, as one would expect. Dom DiMaggio, in a very significant letter to Clark of January 24, 1977, revealed his views:

It is my opinion that major differences between Cronin and McCarthy was leniency. Cronin was lenient and handed over to a more disciplinarian, McCarthy, a team accustomed to Cronin's ways, and a team which found it difficult to change in due course to McCarthy's satisfaction. This, and advancing age, caused what in my belief was McCarthy's unhappy departure.

These remarks obviously generate thoughts as to what is the ideal manager-type and different answers will be provided, depending on the points of view of ownership, players, managers and fans. Fans prefer winners, whatever the managerial methods may be to produce these results. Bill Carrigan had the greatest success, with top-flight teams in his first managerial service but later had cellar experiences with very weak clubs. Jimmy Collins also was a winner until his players grew old and he became the recipient of ownership displeasure. Ed Barrow, without a pro-ball background, did well in 1918 with capable players. What the characteristics of a manager should be, as ownership, players, managers and fans might identify them, would make a very interesting inquiry. This author believes the ideal manager, among his many requisites, should be a little more tough than tender, but understanding of the various differences in the temperament and character of the individual players and of the necessity sometimes of different approaches; however, he must subordinate all this to the welfare and success of the team as a unit.

1948 SEASON

After the 1947 season, Mr. Yawkey directed his prompt attention to lifting the team to a challenging position. From St. Louis, he obtained two good pitchers, Ellis Kinder and Jack Kramer. The moundsmen were further bolstered by Mel Parnell's blossoming into instant success in his first full year, and Bill Goodman's becoming the most valuable utility man in Red Sox history.

Off to an atrocious start, the 1948 team probably lost the pennant in the spring, but actually carried their subsequent late-season surge down to the final 2-game series against the Yankees, which they swept, as the Indians and Tigers divided theirs, causing a tie and the first playoff in American League history. Boston won the toss for the game site, and McCarthy surprised many by sending Denny Galehouse, 8-8, to oppose Gene Beardon, 19-7, and the possessor of the League's best ERA. Although Gene had only one day's rest, he limited Boston to 5 hits and won 8-3, behind solid hitting, featuring Lou Boudreau's two homers, and one by Keltner.

Dom DiMaggio's reevaluation of that season in a letter to Clark of January 24, 1977, included:

> The last two days of 1948 were a source of satisfaction because we did what we had to do—beat the N. Y. Yankees both days while Cleveland had to lose one to Detroit. In the process of beating the Yankees the first game of that two game set, we eliminated them from any chance they may have had. However, the playoff game loss was very disappointing, but hastened my marriage date.

So it went. But for the season, individual accolades went to pitchers Jack Kramer, 18-5, Mel Parnell, 15-8, and Ellis Kinder, 10-7. Jack led the League in winning percentage, Mel was fourth in ERA.

Red Sox batters as usual were prominent. Williams, the League's Most Valuable Player, scored in seven departments: first in batting, slugging average, doubles and walks; third in RBI, total bases and runs (tie). Goodman hit .310; Stephens .269, second in RBI, fourth in total bases and home runs; Doerr .285, fifth in homers; DiMaggio .285, second in runs; and Pesky .281, third in runs (tie).

1949

Lightning may not strike twice in the same place, but for the 1949 Red Sox, after a gallant uphill fight, again coming off a very poor spring start, once more lost the championship by a single game. With a 1-game margin they played and lost the vital concluding 2-game series at Yankee Stadium. Needing only one victory, the Red Sox lost a 4-0 lead and the game in the first day, then went down in the second game, 5-3, as Vic Raschi (20-10) prevailed, supported by a decisive 4-run eighth in which Al Zarilla just missed snagging Jerry Coleman's triple. The breaks of both games went against the Red Sox, but at the same time, full credit must be given the Yankees, who did what their 1904 team had been unable to do against an earlier Boston club.

At least seven Bostons had done very well in the season. Parnell, 25-7, was first in League wins, ERA, complete games and innings, and second in winning percentage. Kinder, 23-6, led in winning percentage and shutouts, was second in wins, third in strikeouts, and fifth in complete games. Ted Williams for the second time was selected Most Valuable Player for placing first in slugging average, total bases, home runs, RBI (tie), doubles, walks and runs, and second in batting and hits. Doerr, .309, placed fourth in RBI and slugging average, and fifth in batting; DiMaggio, .307, third in hits, doubles and runs; Pesky, .306; Goodman, .298; and Stephens .270, first (tie) in RBI, and second in homers, slugging average and total bases.

1950

The 1950 Sox did not lose the pennant by a single game, but by four, as their season's record was 94-60 for a .610 percentage, the latter not surpassed by a Red Sox team since that time. The Yankees were the champions with the Tigers one game closer than Boston. Boston, for the third consecutive year, had a poor beginning, and their offensive power was dealt a heavy blow when Ted Williams, fielding a ball in the All-Star game at Chicago, broke his elbow, emphasizing at least to Red Sox fans the inherent dangers that lurk within the All-Star game concepts. There were some unusual seasonal achievements, such as the team having 7 pitchers better than .500, but only Parnell, 18-10, markedly exceeded his defeats with victories. Club batting was ferocious, .302, with Billy Goodman the batting champion at .354, DiMaggio, .328, Zarilla, .325, Dropo, .322, Williams .317 for

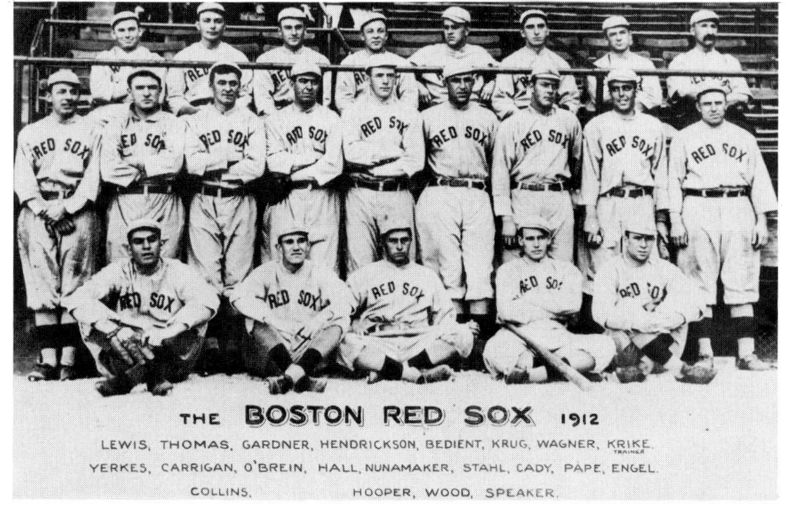

BOSTON 1912 WORLD CHAMPIONS. Over the years, of the nine pennant-winning Boston Red Sox teams, 1912's was the one most frequently photographed. One reason for this was the fact that they clinched the championship early, winning by the handsome margin of 14 games. In this period of American sports history, postcards frequently were issued, including those of the ball parks; today, these are rare, desirable collector's items. Doubtless the presence of so many well-liked stars on the Boston team aided the sales distribution of this card.

SHOW YOUR COLORS! ROOT FOR BOSTON! When World Series time arrives, there are a variety of specially produced-for-the-occasion pennants and buttons for those who wish to visibly identify their loyalties and also to have tangible pleasant memories of a fine season. The elaborate 1916 Boston Royal Rooters' badge was in keeping with the Boston support of the team by a formal and dedicated organization. Today, and since 1968, the justly famous BoSox Club provides luncheons, speeches, special trips, training for talented area youngsters, and other services on behalf of Boston baseball.

VAUDEVILLE ANYONE?

See page 42 for Duffy Lewis's description of his famous catch off Gabby Cravath in the 1915 World Series at Fenway Park. Lewis's great hitting and fielding made him the deserved hero of the Series. This well-liked and articulate native Californian quickly was signed to a vaudeville contract in his native state. Obviously, the love of the game was not everything in this era. Star players were very happy to earn an extra thousand dollars. From 1911-1913, three Boston Red Sox, Bradley, McHale, and O'Brien, sang on B. F. Keith's famous circuit during the off-season.

When I was in vaudeville they used to ask me questions. I played in San Francisco then Oakland Sacramento and San Diego. In Los Angeles a man asked me in what park did you make that catch off Cravath I told him it was Braves Field he said that was a big field wasn't it I said yes. Bakers Bowl was the name of the Phila Park. Very small park. He said if he hit that ball in Bakers Bowl he would be doing the act instead of you. I had a lot of fun.

"Duffy"

Cravath lived in Los Angeles

RED SOX 1915 WORLD CHAMPIONS. One of the outstanding baseball teams, for which Foster, Shore, Ruth and Leonard won 70 games. The season also marked the sixth and final one for the greatest defensive outfield in the entire history of major-league baseball: Hooper-Speaker-Lewis. The former evaluated the club to the author: "I think our 1915 team was one of the greatest teams in baseball, with the best pitching staff and the best defensive outfield. We played for one run—tried to get on the scoreboard first and then to increase our lead." They also were the first Red Sox club to win a World Championship in only five games.

EVERETT SCOTT — BOSTON RED SOX' OUTSTANDING FIELDER-SHORTSTOP. Everett served Boston during 1914-1921, and for 6 consecutive seasons, 1916-1921, he led the League at his position. He continued his superlative career with the New York Yankees for two years thereafter. Doubtless, typesetters of the annual official League fielding statistics were tempted to set his name ahead of time at the top of the list. A very durable player, Scott still holds the Boston consecutive games record. A master at precise timing, he seldom hurried his throws to first base and frequently his relays would arrive there just a split second ahead of the runner.

GEORGE WHITEMAN, THE MAN WHO NEVER GAVE UP. Many people, including ball players, are subject both to impatience and discouragement. Instant success, although a very pleasant dream, seldom is to be confused with reality. Whiteman had a superabundance of patience, determination and faith in himself. Appearing in only 3 games for the 1907 Bostons, then in 11 more for the 1913 Highlanders, George spent the rest of his baseball time in the minors up to 1918. His delayed chance came in 1918 with the Red Sox, as related in this book, and he lived up to his own convictions by deservedly being selected hero of the 1918 World Series, at the advanced rookie age of 35.

OUR 1918 WORLD CHAMPIONS—WHEN WILL WE HAVE ANOTHER? Harry Hooper, team captain, wrote the name captions. Whitehead should read Whiteman. Harry Frazee is on the extreme left, rear row. It is said that no team picture of this club ever included all the members. In obvious contrast to earlier group photographs of the Bostons of 1903, 1904, 1912, 1915, and 1916, the absence of lettering on the shirts makes this one less effective. This distinguished team represented the end of the Golden Age at Fenway Park, wherein, from 1912 through 1918, four pennants and World Champion flags flew from the flagpole. 28 years would elapse before another pennant.

William D. Eckert

January 7, 1966

Captain Ellery H. Clark, Jr.
United States Naval Reserve
Twenty-five Franklin Street
Annapolis, Maryland

Dear Captain Clark:

Thank you for your letter of December 28th.

Commissioner Frick has turned over correspondence to me relating to the 1918 Red Sox. Included in this were letters from you.

I appreciate your sincere interest in the matter and admire your efforts to assist these men. I would certainly be happy, personally, if I could resolve the matter in their favor.

I am sure you can appreciate the difficulties in thoroughly reviewing something that happened almost fifty years ago. It is difficult for me to understand how, if an injustice had been done, it would not have been corrected earlier. I have, however, obtained and looked at files containing letters of the National Commission at that time and have considered the material you submitted.

I have not had an opportunity to study all of this thoroughly, but would not feel qualified to pass on the merits of these cases at this late date from the information I have.

I appreciate your writing to me and thank you for your good wishes.

Sincerely,

W. D. Eckert

W DE/pm

Commissioner of Baseball

THE APPEAL WAS TURNED DOWN. But to this very day, the author believes that belated baseball recognition—the awarding of the usual World Champion rings—should have been made to the few surviving members of the 1918 team or their wives or next of kin. Later player strikes in the 1970s were settled without reprisals on the athletes, but back in 1918, the threatened strike brought about the action discussed in this letter. Hooper tried hard, on behalf of his teammates who never were on a second World Champion team, to obtain the rings, but without success. At the time General Eckert wrote the above letter, Hooper sent one to the author, commenting: "You will notice that I have changed your middle initial from H. to B. This is also a belated effort to rectify a mistake made by your parents when they named you. It is quite evident that it should have been Ellery Bulldog Clark."

JOE HARRIS. A taciturn, determined journeyman outfielder, Joe spent 1922-1925 with the then very depressed Red Sox, averaging a competent .318 for his 3 full seasons in years when the team was hitting .263, .261, and .277—weak performances in the age of the very lively ball, when the League's average team batting was .282, .290, and .292. Twice he led the Red Sox in batting and triples, once in home runs. Ehmke owed his no-hitter to the watchful Harris.

GEORGE HENRY BURNS. "Tioga" George played first base during 1922-1923 for a .317 average and in 1923 topped the team in hits, doubles, and RBI. Burns was a fine clutch hitter and the author well remembers, even after 54 years, dashing out of Fenway to retrieve his extra-inning game-winning home run in 1923, which had come to a temporary rest on the old embankment, long since removed. Speaking of rest, the National Casket Company used to have an office on the approximate spot.

JACK QUINN. A 1922-1925 Red Sox pitcher, he eventually went on to perform for 21 years and 6 major-league clubs. There were at least two reasons for Jack's durability: his very easy motion and effective spitball. His Boston record of 45-54 was very creditable, considering the almost prone position of the team in his years—3 lasts and 1 seventh-place finish. At age 49, he was still pitching—for the Reds. Red Sox home uniforms were as drab as the team in general, and they had matching scorecards, far unlike the splendid ones of Vice President Gene Kirby in recent years.

PHIL TODT. A relatively long-tenured (1924-1930) Red Sox first baseman in a period when players came and went in quick succession, indicating the perilous posture of the club. Phil deservedly was one of the very few Bostons of this era to make the distribution list of amusement park baseball cards. For 6 seasons, he was the golden glove of the infield: 5 times over .990 and in 1928 making only 5 errors in 1,585 total chances for a League-leading .997. Todt also was a team 4-time leader in home runs, and a 2-time leader in triples and RBI.

IKE BOONE. A 1923-1925 Red Sox right fielder, Ike provided for a mixture of spectator emotions. In 1925, he was defensively at the bottom of his position in League fielding statistics and sometimes had considerable problems with the right field area, leading some witnesses to wonder whether he was trying to catch or elude certain drives. At bat, he was very authoritative, hitting .333 and .330, and twice being team leader in batting and RBI. A friendly, likeable man, he was a firm favorite of the old bleacher and pavilion small crowds.

ED MORRIS. As told on other pages, Ed's life was filled with tragedy, although he enjoyed his own pattern. This most promising strong-armed fast baller won 19 games for the inept 1928 Red Sox, who managed only 57 wins in the entire season, and the next year, he was a very creditable 14-14. Rumors grew that he would be passed along to the Yankees, as had happened to Ruffing and MacFayden. But an arm injury incurred in St. Louis, declining effectiveness, and his death by stabbing in a Florida party-brawl terminated what had seemed to be the beginning of a brilliant career.

TOM OLIVER. From 1930-1933, this fine transition center fielder was defensively in the very highest Red Sox tradition, topping the League in 1930 at .982 and in 1931 with .993. His speed and strong arm also led to his making the most League outfield putouts, 433, and assists, 15, in 1931. Preceded by the also very popular Ira Flagstead (1923-1929), Oliver made many history-minded Boston fans recall the Immortal Outfield of 1910-1915.

ROY JOHNSON. One of the leaders of the early Yawkey years, Roy divided his 1932-1935 seasons about equally between right and left field. His strong arm enabled him to average 15 assists during 3 of those campaigns. As the photograph indicates, he was a great woodsman and consistently effective hitter. Interestingly, he and John Pesky now share fifth place in all-time Red Sox career batting, at a fine .313. His brother Bob later played in the Red Sox outfield of 1944-1945.

BOB DOERR. Without an equal in the 76-year history of the club, Bob for 14 years (1937-1951) typified all the best essentials of a great second baseman: brilliant fielding, quick reflexes, dependable hard-hitting, durability, determination and loyalty. At the end of his active playing days, he had the distinction of being the team's first base coach in championship 1967. To this day, he is among the Red Sox career leaders in 11 batting categories, including third in RBI, third in games, at bats, hits, doubles, home runs, runs, total bases and extra base hits.

BOSTON RECORD			
ear	BH	HR	Ave
937	33	2	224
938	147	5	289
939	167	12	318
940	172	22	291
941	141	16	282
942	158	15	290
943	163	16	270
944	152	15	325
946	158	18	271
947	145	17	258
948	150	27	285
949	167	18	309
950	172	27	294
951	116	13	289

BOSTON RECORD		
Year	BH	Ave
1940	126	301
1941	165	283
1942	178	286
1946	169	316
1947	145	283
1948	185	285
1949	186	307
1950	193	328
1951	189	296
1952	143	294
1953	1	333

DOM DiMAGGIO. Serving Boston with great distinction for 11 seasons (during 1940-1953), outfielder DiMaggio as a player was highly intelligent, modest, talented, dedicated and a fine team man. His success in later life has proven the value of the extended projection of these most desirable personal qualities. Dom holds the club seasonal record for longest hitting streak, 34 games, in 1949, and also for the most seasonal at bats for a Boston right-hander, 648, in 1948. As is true of so many major-league ball players of his vintage, the war-interrupted years provide speculation as to what greater heights careers would otherwise have extended.

89 games, Pesky .312, and Tebbetts .310. A retreat in team achievement was about to begin, with the first stage a modest one, 1951 through 1958, and then a prolonged departure from the front lines, 1959 through 1966. By coincidence, each retreat was of 8 years' duration.

Table 24

RED SOX RETREATS, 1951-1966

Year	Position	Won	Lost	Games Behind	Team Pitching	Team Batting
1951	3	87	67	11	4	3
1952	6	76	78	19	5	3
1953	4	84	69	16	3	4
*1954	4	69	85	42	7	3
1955	4	84	70	12	4	3
1956	4	84	70	13	5	2
1957	3	82	72	16	5	2
1958	3	79	75	13	6	5
1959	5	75	79	19	6	5
1960	7	65	89	32	8	3
**1961	6	76	86	33	8	5
1962	8	72	90	19	9	4
1963	7	76	85	28	9	2
1964	8	72	90	27	9	1
1965	9	62	100	40	9	2
1966	9	72	90	26	10	4

*Even with this won-lost record, the team finished in fourth place.
**One division, 10-club League from 1961 through remainder of period.

SEVEN MANAGERS, 1951-1966

Not necessarily an indication of good fortune, and yet, by coincidence, in close conformity with the overall Boston average of limited managership tenure, seven pilots, O'Neill, Boudreau, Higgins, Jurges, Pesky, Herman and player-manager Runnels for the final 16 games of 1966, all served. Higgins four times aided the club to first-division achievements, Boudreau twice, O'Neill once. None of the group, according to a sampling of players and fans, appeared to have unusual leadership talents. Club pitching was below par, batting above average; but the latter did not counterbalance or outweigh the influence of their lack of mound depth and effectiveness.

Over these seasons, Boston ERA averaged between sixth and seventh place, whereas in batting they placed third. Only in three of the better years, 1951, 1953 and 1955, did the pitching status exceed that of the hitters. As the following tables clearly indicate, the net effect of some good but limited individual mound performances, considerable ability and depth in batting, and average managership yielded the pattern of an average team finish of between fifth and sixth place. Nobody in Boston was particularly pleased with this, and the sudden reversal in combined team dedication, effort and performance under new managership in 1967 caught many Red Sox fans by delighted surprise. Their main opposition, who had not suspected the Boston club would put it all together so quickly, were also surprised at Boston's rise, even if the rise to first would not be gained until the final day.

1951 DEATH OF EDDIE COLLINS

1951 spring training at Sarasota produced one very sad note; in Peter Bent Brigham Hospital, Boston, Vice President Eddie Collins died. For 18 years, he had contributed much to the rise of the Red Sox, including signing two of their greatest stars, Ted Williams and Bob Doerr. As quoted in the *Boston Herald,* March 25, 1951, the day following Mr. Collins's passing:

Ted Williams:

> He has always been on my side ever since he signed me to a Red Sox contract. Whenever I've been in trouble he has talked to me like a father and given me good advice. . . . he always gave me the type of encouragement I needed.

Bob Doerr:

> Eddie always took pride in the fact that I have been able to play second base the past 14 years . . . I was only an 18-year-old kid when Eddie looked me over.

RED SOX SELECTED STATS, 1951-1966

1951	**Pitching**	**Notable League Achievement**
	Kinder, 11-2	First in Saves and Games Pitched
	Parnell, 18-11	
	McDermott, 8-8	Fifth in Saves
	Batting	
	Williams, .318	First in Slugging Average, Total Bases and Walks; Second in RBI and Home Runs; Third in Runs; Fourth in Batting
	Pesky, .313	
	Stephens, .300	
	DiMaggio, .296	First in Runs, Second in Hits, Fifth in Total Bases

(Doerr's last season, Pesky's last full season)

Bobbie Doerr (1937-1951): Outstanding Offensive-Defensive Leader

Considering Doerr's 14 seasons with the Red Sox as a fine team man, and the well-known offensive and defensive consistent performance of this career .288 hitter, there is no question that he ranks as their best second baseman. Three times American League fielder at his position, he also, for Boston, made a grand total of 1,478 double plays, 5 times being most proficient in that category. His career:

Table 25

AMERICAN LEAGUE SEASONAL PERFORMANCES

Category	Position in Category (Number of Times)				
	1	2	3	4	5
Slugging Average	1			1	
Triples	1				
Batting		1			1
RBI				2	2
Total Bases				1	1
Home Runs					1
Totals	2	1	0	4	5

Table 26

BOSTON ALL-TIME CAREER BATTING

Category	Position	Achievement
Games	3	1,865
At Bats	3	7,093
Hits	3	2,042
RBI	3	1,247
Total Bases	3	3,270
Runs	3	1,094
Extra Base Hits	3	693
Doubles	3	381
Home Runs	3	223
Triples	4	89

1952	**Batting**	**Notable League Achievement**
	Kell, .319	
	Goodman, .306	
	Lipon, .205	Shortstop Fielding Leader.

(Williams after 6 games went on active duty in the Korean War; last seasons for DiMaggio and Stephens, first for Delock)

1953	**Pitching**	**Notable League Achievement**
	Parnell, 21-8	Second in Wins, Third in Winning Percentage, Fourth in Strikeouts
	McDermott, 18-10	
	Kinder, 10-6	First in Saves and Games Pitched
	Batting	
	Goodman, .313	Third in Batting
	Kell, .307	Second in Doubles and Third Base Fielding Leader
	Piersall, .272	Third in Triples
	White, .273	Third in Doubles

Dom DiMaggio (1940-1953)

The DiMaggio family—Joe, Dom and Vince—spent a total of 34 years in the major leagues. Though brother Joe generally was recognized as the best of the trio, Dom was an outstanding Boston star, provoking the famous line in the Red Sox song, "Who'sa better than his brother Joe?" His distinguished career:

Table 27

AMERICAN LEAGUE SEASONAL PERFORMANCE

Category	Placement in Category (Number of Times)				
	1	2	3	4	5
Runs	2	2	3		
Triples	1				
Stolen Bases	1				
Hits			2		
Batting			1		1
Doubles			1		
Total Bases				1	1
Totals	4	2	7	1	2

Table 28

BOSTON ALL-TIME CAREER BATTING

Category	Position	Achievement
Doubles	4	308
Total Bases	4	2,363
Runs	4	1,046
At Bats	5	5,640
Hits	5	1,680
Extra Base Hits	5	452
Games	6	1,399
RBI	10	618

1954	Pitching	Notable League Achievement
	Sullivan, 15-12 (First full season)	
	Kinder, 8-8	Second in Saves and Games
	Brewer, 10-9 (First full season)	

Batting

Williams, .345 (First season after return from Korean War, then broke shoulder in spring training, playing in only 117 games)	First in Slugging Average and Walks, Second in Home Runs
Jensen, .276 (First season with Red Sox)	First in Stolen Bases, Third in RBI, Fourth in Home Runs
Goodman, .294	Second in Walks, Third in Doubles

Death of Harry Agganis, 1955

For the first and only time to date in Red Sox history, on June 27, 1955, at Sancta Maria Hospital, they lost an active player. On that date, a lung embolism took the life of their very promising first baseman, Harry Agganis. He had been the greatest all-around athlete in the history of Boston University and "the Golden Greek," as he affectionately was called, was expected to become another in a great line of Boston first basemen. Batting .313 when forced by illness from the Red Sox lineup in early June, millions were shocked at his tragic death. Mr. Yawkey observed, "The news of Harry Agganis's death has stunned and saddened both Mrs. Yawkey and myself. The Red Sox . . . have lost a young athlete of outstanding ability and character."

1956	Pitching	Notable League Achievement
	Brewer, 19-9	Fifth in Winning Percentage
	Sullivan, 14-7	
	Delock, 13-7	Fourth in Saves
	Parnell, 7-6	No-hitter against Chicago, July 14
	(His last season)	
	Batting	
	Williams, .345	Second in Batting and Slugging Average, Third in Walks
	Jensen, .315	First in Triples, Third in Total Bases, Fifth in Stolen Bases
	Vernon, .310	
	Piersall, .293	First in Doubles, Center Field Fielding Leader
1957	Pitching	Notable League Achievement
	Brewer, 16-13	Third in Wins and Complete Games
	Sullivan, 14-11	Fourth in Complete Games, Fifth in ERA
	Delock, 9-8	Third in Saves
	Batting	
	Williams, .388	First in Batting and Slugging Average, Second in Home Runs and Walks, Third in Total Bases
	Malzone, .292	Second in Hits, Third (tie) in RBI and Doubles, Fifth in Total Bases, Third Base Fielding Leader
	(First full season)	
	Jensen, .281	Third (tie) in RBI
	Piersall, .261	Third in Runs

1958	**Pitching**	**Notable League Achievement**
	Delock, 14-8	
	Sullivan, 13-9	
	Kiely, 5-2	Third in Saves
	Wall, 8-9	Fourth in Saves
	Fornieles, 8-7 (First full season for Boston)	
	Batting	
	Jensen, .286	League's Most Valuable Player, First in RBI, Second in Walks, Fifth in Home Runs and Total Bases
	Williams, .325	First in Batting, Third in Walks, Fourth in Slugging Average
	Runnels, .322	Second in Batting and Runs
	Malzone, .295	Second in Hits
1959	**Pitching**	**Notable League Achievement**
	Delock, 11-6	
	Casale, 13-8	
	Fornieles, 5-3	Fifth in Saves
	Batting	
	Runnels, .314	Second in Walks, Third in Batting and Hits
	Malzone, .280	Second in Doubles
	Jensen, .277	First in RBI, Third in Stolen Bases
1960	**Pitching**	**Notable League Achievement**
	Monbouquette, 14-11 (First full season)	
	Fornieles, 10-5	First in Saves and Games
	Batting	
	Runnels, .320	First in Batting, Second Base Fielding Leader
	Williams, .316 (final season)	Home Run last time at bat
	Wertz, .282	Third in RBI

The Ted Williams Era (1939-1960)

If it is reasonable to have identified earlier Red Sox years, such as 1901-1908 and 1909-1920, as the ages of Cy Young and Harry Hooper, respectively, it is very reasonable to select the name of Ted Williams as representative of the much longer period 1939-1960.

Williams's stature as a player dominates all other Boston hitters both in excellence and longevity. One can only speculate on what his additional achievements would have been had he not served in two wars and sustained two crippling ball field injuries. If and when the art and science of batting should become recognized by academicians, Ted Williams will be in the front row of honorary degree recipients.

As to the tangibles, the following capsule table provides essential information.

Table 29

TED WILLIAMS, 1939-1960

	All-time Red Sox Position	Career Total	American League Seasonal Leadership Position				
			1	2	3	4	5
Slugging Average	1	634	9	1	1	2	
Walks	1	2018	8	2	2		
Batting	1	.344	6	3	1	1	
Runs	1	1798	6	1	2		
Total Bases	1	4884	6		4		
Home Runs	1	521	4	4	2		
RBI	1	1839	4	2	1	1	1
Doubles	1	525	2	2			
Hits	1	2654		1	2		
Triples	7	71					
Extra base hits	1	1117					
Games	2	2292					
At bats	2	7706					
Totals			45	16	15	4	1

Most Valuable Player, 1946 and 1949
Last major-league batter over .400—.406 in 1941

As to the intangibles, it is semi-tragic that Williams, who has very keen eyesight and hearing and is a sensitive person, as most of us are, was justifiably upset at certain members of the Boston press and certain insulting spectators. Dave Egan, Mel Webb and Hy Hurwitz never came close to making his private list of most admired people, directly opposite to his feelings about Mr. Yawkey, Eddie Collins and writer George Carens.

Perhaps the joys and sorrows, moments of calm and ire, all were summed up and contained in the few seconds immediately following Ted's last-time-at-bat home run at Fenway Park. In his autobiography, he vividly portrayed his mixed emotions and his delight at receiving the most enthusiastic and sustained ovation ever in the history of Boston baseball, going back to Al Spalding, the baseball Wright brothers and the original Boston Red Stockings of 1871.

But Ted mentally and emotionally talked himself out of doffing his cap as he jogged around the bases for the last time. His earlier frustrations and not-yet-healed emotional wounds would not permit him to make a final and possibly magnificent gesture. All things considered, the author admires Ted Williams in many, many ways and feels his decision not to tip his cap was in full keeping with the man and the sincerity behind his judgment. If more people had at least tried to apply the Golden Rule to Ted, everyone involved would have been both happier and better. Williams, as long as baseball is played, will be remembered for his accomplishments and multi-faceted characteristics, one of which, his Jimmy Fund support, marks him as a very great humanitarian, aiding in the fight against cancer in children.

1961	Pitching	Notable League Achievement
	Schwall, 15-7	Fifth in Winning Percentage
	Fornieles, 9-8	Third in Saves
	Batting	
	Runnels, .317	First Base Fielding Leader
	Yastrzemski, .266 (First season)	
	Schilling, .259	Second Base Fielding Leader
1962	Pitching	Notable League Achievement
	Wilson, 12-8	No-hitter, June 26, against Los Angeles
	Monbouquette, 15-13	No-hitter, August 1, at Chicago
	Conley, 15-14	
	Radatz, 9-6 (First Boston season)	First in Saves and Games
	Batting	
	Runnels, .326	First in Batting
	Yastrzemski, .296	Second in Doubles, Fourth in Total Bases
	Clinton, .294	Second in Triples
	Bressoud, .277	Third in Doubles

1963	Pitching	Notable League Achievement
	Monbouquette, 20-10	Third in Innings, Fourth in Wins
	Radatz, 15-6	Second in Saves and Games, Third in Winning Percentage
	Batting	
	Yastrzemski, .321	First in Batting, Hits, Doubles and Walks
	Stuart, .261	First in RBI and Total Bases, Second in Home Runs, Fourth in Slugging Average

1964	Pitching	Notable League Achievement
	Radatz, 16-9	First in Saves, Second in Games
	Batting	
	Bressoud, .293	Second in Doubles
	Stuart, .279	Second in RBI, Fifth in Home Runs and Total Bases

(The team did not have a single regular who hit .300, but the club was the League's team batting leader at .258)

1965	Pitching	Notable League Achievement
	Morehead, 10-18	No-hitter against Cleveland, September 16
	Radatz, 9-11	Fifth in Saves
	Batting	
	Yastrzemski, .312	First in Slugging Average, Second in Batting and Doubles
	Mantilla, .275	Third in Walks, Fourth in RBI
	Tony Conigliaro, .269	First in Home Runs, Second in Slugging Average, Fifth in Total Bases

1966	Batting	Notable League Achievement
	Yastrzemski, .278	First in Doubles
	Foy, .262	Second in Walks

(For second time in three seasons the club did not have a regular at .300. Only two batters in the League were over .300)

FIVE RED SOX STARS SHARE MEMORIES
AND EMOTIONS, 1939-1962

In personal letters to the author, five selected Boston heroes, Ted Williams, Pete Runnels, Jim Piersall, Mel Parnell and Bill Monbouquette, graciously furnished particularly valuable insights into their personalities and judgments and continued the kindness of earlier Red Sox stars who provided similar personal material in order to assist the novel and major themes of this volume.

Williams to Clark, July 22, 1954:

Perhaps the most memorable incident was the day Eddie Collins saw me in San Diego and obtained an option on my services from Mr. Lane. After all that was really what brought me to Boston and the Red Sox, and to all the fines [*sic*] things that have happened to me since.

Runnels to Clark, undated letter:

It's hard for me to overlook the two batting titles I won. But I guess the one I lost was the one I had the most fun in. I lost to Ted Williams on the last day in 1958. I guess I enjoyed that more because of the great competition he offered. He really closed fast on me that last week, but wasn't he capable!

Piersall to Clark, undated letter:

The first time I put on a Red Sox uniform was the biggest thrill. I had dreamed as a young boy playing for the Red Sox. Want to wish you the very best with your book.

Parnell to Clark, July 6, 1974, on his no-hitter of July 14, 1956:

There was nothing in my pre-game warmup that indicated I would have unusual stuff. However that day, July 14, 1956, was a day interrupted by showers. Because of the showers I warmed up three times before the game could get underway, however once we started the weather and the game got better and better. Warmups served only as a loosening up exercise, as it never did indicate to me whether I would or wouldn't have my stuff in a ball game. I recall days of having good stuff warming up but little in the game and vice versa. . . . In my no-hitter . . . I recall having a good sinker and throwing it about eighty per cent of the time.

The closest hit as I recall was a ground ball to the right of Billy Goodman. Billy handled the ball on the run and made a force at second. The hardest hit ball was by Minnie Minoso which went foul into the third base grandstand.

During the game I really never did reach a state of nervousness. I feel the reason for that was because I just didn't expect it to happen. After the game I was nervous as could be, mainly because I couldn't be myself with all of the hullabaloo around me and my realizing what had happened. A few of my teammates showed signs of being nervous mainly because they feared making a bad play and messing up the no-hitter. Jackie Jensen was probably the most affected.

Monbouquette to Clark, undated letter on his August 1, 1962, no-hitter:

> I recall while I was working the kinks out while warming up I felt very loose for a cool night and I was popping the ball and had very good rhythm. After all I had not won a game in 56 days. . . . I was most nervous when I went out to start the last of the 8th inning because when we had scored in the top of the inning to break the scoreless tie and plus I was pitching against Early Wynn. The closest hit was off the bat of Charlie Maxwell who hit a line drive into right center but the right fielder got back in time. I believe it was the hardest hit ball all night.

1967-1968 SEASONS: A SECOND YAWKEY PENNANT BUT NO REPEATER

Table 30

Year	Position	Won	Lost	Net Gain or Loss in Games over Previous Season	ERA	Batting
1966	9	72	90	−10	10	4
1967	1	92	70	+20	8	1
1968	4	86	76	− 6	8	33

"The Impossible Dream" aided by the very popular dramatization of Cervantes's *Don Quixote* and its smash-hit song became the lasting allusion to this significant Red Sox pennant year of 1967. It was and to this date has remained the most inspirational year in Boston American League history. Indicative of the protracted closeness of the race, four teams eventually finished only 3 games apart while but one separated the top three. Quite obviously, the Red Sox percentage established a new League record for lowest championship average, .568. Nobody in Boston was particularly upset by this statistical discovery.

Examining first some of the usual stats to gain a partial insight into the results, we find the following:

Table 31

Team	Won	Lost	ERA	Batting	Total RBIs, First 6 Regulars
Boston	92	70	3.36	.255	446
Minnesota	91	71	3.14	.240	421
Detroit	91	71	3.32	.243	417
Chicago	89	73	2.45	.225	283

On an individual performance basis, there was more difference than in the team stats. Boston had the winning seasonal double—Jim Lonborg and Carl Yastrzemski. Jim, Cy Young Award winner, was League's best in victories and strikeouts, second in winning percentage, complete games and innings, and won the final game. Carl, the American League's Most Valuable Player, was an offensive giant: first in batting, runs batted in, total bases, slugging average and runs; tied for first in home runs; third in doubles.

Jose Santiago, 12-4, Gary Bell, 12-8, and Lee Stange, 8-10, but with the best ERA of any Red Sox starter, together with John Wyatt, 10-7 and 20 saves, gave the team sufficient pitching depth to do the job right. On the Boston attack, George Scott finished fourth in League batting at .303 and drove in 82 runs (Yaz had scored 121 with his bat); Tony Conigliaro, 67 (his season ended during his ninety-fifth game when he was seriously injured in an eye by a pitched ball); Petrocelli, 66; Reggie Smith, 61; and Joe Foy, 49.

A basic theme of this book is that the intangibles are strong factors and probably determinants when the competition is close. It is felt by this author, though admittedly it cannot really be measured and proved as if in a chemistry laboratory, that the 1967 Red Sox had more desire and determination as a team to win than did their rivals. Roaring crowds at Fenway reached 1,727,832 for a new seasonal record. On the road and inside and outside New England, the Red Sox became popular favorites, as deserving underdogs, and attracted many rooters including a good many fans who up to that season had been only casual followers.

When, on October 1, Boston had at least gained a tie for the championship, and before California later the same day would knock Detroit out of the race, Red Sox management, players and fans let their emotions out—Tom Yawkey, Executive Vice President and General Manager Dick O'Connell (to be selected Major League Executive of the Year in 1967 and again in 1975), Manager Dick Williams, Yaz, Lonborg and all the others. Inside the park, Jim Lonborg was carried off the field in triumph, his sleeve and buttons ripped off by the surging crowd. Other zealots quickly dismantled the scoreboard. Outside, Boston policemen jumped for joy and threw their caps into the air. One enthusiast in his exhilaration fell down a freight elevator shaft. It was a moment of Boston parochial emotionalism at its very best. National radio and TV interrupted programs to pass the news to all hands, "The Boston Red Sox have won the American League pennant."

The Red Sox successfully had put together both the intangibles and tangibles of baseball to their own delight and that of millions of others. Three members of the team later provided the author with their happy memories of that great moment:

Jim Lonborg to Clark undated letter:

> As I look back over my career with the Red Sox there can be only one most pleasant memory. It happened on a Sunday, the 1st of October, 1967, when the Red Sox played the Minnesota Twins for what turned out to be the American League Championship. It was a most memorable day in that I was the winning pitcher, had been carried on the shoulders of some of America's finest fans and was able to share a moment of history with a group of people who so deserved the honor of being American League champs.

Carl Yastrzemski to Clark, January 29, 1974:

> . . . concerning my greatest moment as a Red Sox player, I feel that it must have been when we won the Pennant in 1967 while coming from eighth place and since it had not been won by us since 1946.

It was not only the greatest moment as a team member but also my greatest individual moment since it was that year that I won the Triple Crown.

Lee Stange to Clark, March 14, 1974:

I think anyone who was at Fenway Park the last day of the 1967 season will never forget it. To me it was a dream come true and something I had dreamed about for a long time. I guess since I was a very young boy.

Another thing that was very satisfying to me was to see the greatest fans in baseball really having something to celebrate. There's no doubt in my mind that the fans at Fenway had quite a bit to do with our winning.

Larry Claflin of the *Boston Herald,* official *Sporting News* correspondent for the Red Sox, commented in *The Official Baseball Guide for 1968:*

There was more to Red Sox success than the fans, however. Luck was a part of it, and so was rookie Manager Dick Williams, whose sarcastic, brawling Gashouse style won him Manager-of-the-Year honors. . . . Williams kept his players fighting for the right to play all year, and that unquestionably was a factor in success.*

With hopes of gaining the first Boston World Championship since 1918, and having the advantage of being sentimental favorites, should that be an important factor, the team took the field on October fourth, as the Red Sox band played "For Boston."

1967 WORLD SERIES

Table 32

Team	Won	Lost	ERA	K	BB	Hits	SB	RBI	Runs	Batting
St. Louis	4	3	2.66	30	17	51	7	24	25	.223
Boston	3	4	3.39	49	17	49	1	19	21	.216

---

*Extracts from *The Official Baseball Guide* (1968, 1970, and 1976), reprinted by permission of the *Sporting News,* St. Louis, Missouri 63132.

Table 33
SERIES' BATTING LEADERS

Name	Team	Hits	RBI	Runs	SB	Batting
Brock	St. Louis	12	3	8	7	.414
*Yastrzemski	Boston	10	5	4		.400
Jones	Boston	7	1	2		.389
Maris	St. Louis	10	7	3		.385
Javier	St. Louis	9	4	9		.360
Andrews	Boston	4	1	2		.308

*Defensive outfield star of Series; threw out two advancing runners and made three fine catches.

Table 34
SERIES' LEADING PITCHERS

Name	Team	GS	CG	IP	H	R	ER	SO	BB	W	L	ERA
Gibson	St. Louis	3	3	27	14	4	3	26	5	3	0	1.00
Lonborg	Boston	3	2	24	14	8	7	11	2	2	1	2.63

Obviously, the cold statistics of these tables reveal much significance in the analysis of the St. Louis victory and Boston defeat. But they do not reveal the background influence of two very important factors that materially aided the Cardinals. Much earlier, on July 15, a smoking line drive off Roberto Clemente's bat had broken pitcher Bob Gibson's right leg, and he was out for 52 days. But the leg healed without complications and Bob, being groomed for the Series, had five starts near the end of the regular season. St. Louis clinched their flag on September 18 and no fatal staleness developed. In contrast, the Red Sox, having to pitch Lonborg on the final day of their season, with the Series scheduled to begin October fourth, could not assign their ace the desired rotation for games 1-4-7. But Gibson was ready for this perfect sequence and he made most effective use of it, emerging a three-time winner and the hero of the Series. He prevailed in the opener, 2-1, yielding 6 hits, then progressively got better, taking the fourth, 6-0 on a 5-hitter, and the decisive seventh, 7-3, limiting Boston to 3 safeties.

Meanwhile, after Santiago had been nipped in the opener in which the Red Sox' only score had been his home run, Lonborg took the second with a 1-hit, 5-0 shutout, and the fifth at

St. Louis, 3-1, with just 3 hits off his baffling pitching. Returning to Fenway, and aided by 6-inning home runs by Yaz, Smith and Petrocelli, Wyatt, in relief of rookie Waslewski, prevailed 8-4, tying the Series. But in the final, weary Jim Lonborg, pounded for 10 hits and 6 runs, left the game after the top half of the sixth to a sustained standing ovation of the Boston crowd.

Some 6 years later, Rico Petrocelli reflected upon these stirring events:

Petrocelli to Clark, January 21, 1974:

> My greatest thrill in baseball so far has been the 1967 World Series. Playing in a world series in only my third year in the major leagues was the most exciting moment I have spent in the nine years I've been a ball player. The sixth game in particular was a thrill for me because I hit two home runs and we won the ball game. We lost the seventh game to a great pitcher and a great team, Bob Gibson and the Cardinals. . . . I didn't realize how tough it was to get to the World Series but the next five years convinced me.

Conclusions: Boston momentum had not carried over from the final week of the regular season to the Series. Events had favored Bob Gibson over Jim Lonborg. The Red Sox' emotional joy at gaining the pennant was somewhat dimmed by failing for a second time in the Yawkey Years to win a World Championship. But unlike the idealistic, impractical Don Quixote who foolishly had tilted with a windmill, the Red Sox bravely had broken their lance using it to the best of their abilities against real baseball giants, Bob Gibson and his teammates. The Red Sox and their Impossible Dream achievements in the regular season had gained many believers and admirers.

1968

There were 2 main reasons for the Red Sox' decline from 1-game winners in 1967 to 17-game trailers in 1968. One of these received much greater publicity than the other. Injuries helped strike down the Bostons.

In sharp contrast to the generally happy thoughts and events associated with Christmas Eve, on that date in 1967, Lonborg, skiing at Lake Tahoe, severely tore a knee ligament. Following surgery and at least reasonable recovery, he was able to appear in only 113 innings, for a 6-10 record, for a net loss of 16 victories from 1967. Santiago's arm went bad during the summer and he finished at 9-4. Bell and Stange dropped from a combined 24-12 to 16-16. However, newcomers Ray Culp, from the Cubs, and Dick Ellsworth, a Philly graduate, had great seasons, 16-6 and 16-7, respectively. But that was insufficient to place the team any higher than fourth. All-around Detroit power proved decisive. Detroit's first four pitchers gained 71 wins, Boston's a modest 52.

Table 35

1968	Team	Won	Lost	ERA	Batting
	Detroit	103	59	2.71	.235
	Baltimore	91	71	2.66	.225
	Cleveland	86	75	2.66	.234
	Boston	86	76	3.33	.236

The Red Sox' hitting had been unable to overcome their weaker pitching. Baltimore's light batting had failed to support good pitching. Cleveland's top four had won 10 less games than Detroit's. Moreover, Detroit had scored the most runs in the League and yielded the fewest. Thus, the Tigers had well earned and deserved their championship, even if a healthy Jim Lonborg might have made the winning difference for the Bostons.

In Red Sox batting, there were several interesting developments. Tony Conigliaro, after a game try, was unable to make the team because of his continuing eye problem as a result of the injury incurred the previous summer. Yaz was the only American Leaguer to hit over .300, and he won the batting title with .301. Comparing the first 6 Red Sox of 1967 with the first 6 of 1968 in RBI, the later team was only 43 behind, chiefly because of Ken Harrelson's banner season: 109 RBI, 35 home runs, 277 total bases and a slugging average of .518. George Scott dipped badly from .303 and 82 RBI to .171 and 25 and was benched as a consequence. But the years heal, and after being traded to the Brewers, following the 1976 season, Scott was re-acquired by the rebuilding Red Sox. Also, Bernie Carbo, who was traded to the Brewers as well, rejoined the Sox following Boston's disappointing season. Foy, Smith and Andrews improved in RBI, while Rico Petrocelli dropped 20 and Yaz 47. But Yaz was a League standout for the second consecutive season:

First in Batting	.301
First in Walks	119
Second in Runs	90
Third in Doubles	32
Fourth in Total Bases	267
Fourth in Slugging Average	.495

Other honors for the team were obtained by Ken Harrelson leading all right fielders with a perfect 1.000 as a result of 249 chances flawlessly handled and Petrocelli topping all shortstops with his glove and arm, making only 12 seasonal errors. Reggie Smith was first in League doubles, Culp second in winning percentage, Ellsworth fourth, while Stange placed fourth in saves. With mixed emotions, the 1968 Boston crowds, indicating good promotion among main causes, upped the attendance record to a still existing all-time high of 1,940,788. The one-division American League would be no more; beginning in 1969 it would go to a two-division profile, with the two winners engaging in best-of-5 championship series, for the pennant. Boston eventually would make it on the seventh try, confirming some beliefs of wave-watchers that the seventh one, on an incoming tide, will reach the highest mark. 1975 would illustrate this concept.

Table 36

EAST DIVISION, 1969-1974: SECONDS AND THIRDS—A PLATEAU

	Team	Position	Won	Lost	ERA	Batting
1969	Baltimore	1	109	53	2.83	.265
	Boston	3	87	75	3.92	.251
1970	Baltimore	1	108	54	3.15	.257
	Boston	3	87	75	3.87	.261
1971	Baltimore	1	101	57	2.99	.261
	Boston	3	85	77	3.80	.252
1972	Detroit	1	96	70	2.96	.237
	Boston	2	89	73	3.65	.267
1973	Baltimore	1	97	65	3.07	.266
	Boston	2	89	73	3.65	.267
1974	Baltimore	1	91	71	3.27	.256
	Boston	3	84	78	3.72	.264

As indicated, for these 6 seasons, Red Sox consistency was remarkable, varying only a maximum of 5 games in annual victories. But the Orioles took the division titles 5 of these years, while the Tigers, in the strike-delayed 1972 race, nipped the Red Sox by winning 2 of 3 in their final series at Detroit, as Lolich and Fryman prevailed over Curtis and Tiant, respectively. In the years the Orioles won, their pitching advantage over Boston was noticeable, which the Boston batting was unable to overcome. Individual Red Sox players, as usual, stood out.

RED SOX SELECTED STATS, 1969-1974

1969	**Pitching**	**Notable League Achievement**
	Nagy, 12-2	
	Culp, 17-8	
	Siebert, 14-10	
	Lyle, 8-3	Third in Saves and Games
	Batting	
	Smith, .309	Second in Batting and Triples
	Petrocelli, .297	Second in Slugging Average, Fourth in Home Runs (tie) and Doubles (tie), Fifth in Stolen Bases, Shortstop Fielding Leader
	Yastrzemski, .255	Fourth in Home Runs (tie), Fifth in RBI (tie) and Walks
1970	**Pitching**	**Notable League Achievement**
	Peters, 16-11	
	Culp, 17-14	Fifth in Strikeouts and Complete Games
	Siebert, 15-8	Fifth in Winning Percentage
	Batting	
	Yastrzemski, .3286	First in Slugging Average, Total Bases and Runs, Second in Batting and Walks (tie), Third in Home Runs
	Smith, .303	Third in Runs (tie)
	Tony Conigliaro, .266 (Made heroic comeback in 1969)	Second in RBI, Fourth in Home Runs
1971	**Pitching**	**Notable League Achievement**
	Siebert, 16-10	
	Peters, 14-11	
	Lee, 9-2	
	Batting	
	Yastrzemski, .254	Second in Walks
	Petrocelli, .251	Third Base Fielding Leader

1972	**Pitching**	**Notable League Achievement**
	Tiant, 15-6	First in ERA, Third in Winning Percentage
	Pattin, 17-13	
	Curtis, 11-8	
	Lee, 7-4	
	Batting	
	Fisk, .293	First in Triples (tie), Second in Slugging Average
	Harper, .254	Third in Runs
1973	**Pitching**	**Notable League Achievement**
	Tiant, 20-13	Fourth in Complete Games
	Lee, 17-11	Third in ERA
	Moret, 13-2	
1973	**Batting**	**Notable League Achievement**
	Yastrzemski, .296	Third in Walks
	Harper, .281	First in Stolen Bases
1974	**Pitching**	**Notable League Achievement**
	Tiant, 22-13	First in Shutouts, Third in Wins (tie), Fifth in Complete Games
	Lee, 17-15	
	Batting	
	Yastrzemski, .301	First in Runs, Second in Walks

RED SOX MANAGERS, 1959-1964

On September 23, 1969, Dick Williams was fired. In his
freshman year he had led the team to the pennant, followed by
key injuries and a drop to fourth place. Even with a slight improvement during his final, partial season, the club standing did
not adequately reflect the problems that were developing and
increasing. Larry Claflin, writing in *The Official Baseball Guide
for 1970,* summarized major factors in Dick's departure:

Dick Williams, the controversial manager for the past three
seasons was fired. . . . Williams had been waging an uphill fight
with the Red Sox ever since the 1967 World Series. After winning the '67 pennant as a rookie manager and with limited
pitching, Williams had nothing but hard luck. . . . There were
myriad . . . disciplinary problems for Williams. The chief one
concerned Carl Yastrzemski. . . . In August, Williams fined Yaz
$500 for 'loafing on the field' and the morale problems of the
Red Sox became even more obvious. . . . Gradually it became

obvious that the Red Sox must get rid of either the manager or the players who were openly opposed to him. The front office fired Williams with a few days left on the schedule, blaming his 'lack of communication' with the players.

Coach Eddie Popowski guided the club in the remaining few games, then Eddie Kasko was hired as manager, serving 4 seasons, 1970-1973. His detailed analysis of the complexities of this office, increasing with the years, follows:

Letter of Eddie Kasko to Clark of February 1, 1977:

When I took the job managing the Red Sox in 1970, I felt the only way to win and accomplish the job for the Red Sox was to try to maintain a dedicated attitude by each and every player. They had to act as a single solid unit. This was harder to accomplish as the years went on, and I imagine it is a near impossible task today.

Let me preface my observations by remembering the player-manager relationship when I was a player. Then the manager almost had dictatorial powers. What he said was law. The prime reason being fear. Fear of losing a starting job, fear of fines, or fear of being sent to the minors. The manager had a 'hammer.'

I felt a change taking place when I started managing. There was more managing 'off the field' in order to maintain a feeling of spirit and unity on the field. Today, as I said before, it must be a near impossible task. Blame it on a looser society, higher salaries, or fewer minor leagues, a situation that forces players into the major leagues at an earlier age with less experience, or something else. The fact is, attitudes have changed. The weapons in a manager's arsenal are slowly disappearing. Fines wind up as a grievance before the players' association, demotion to the minor leagues is out of the question for various reasons, and benching a regular as a form of discipline is out of the question. Player contracts as a whole are longer and for more money than a manager's, which creates a difficult situation.

My approach to managing the Red Sox was to try to bring out the personal pride in each player. If a player has pride in himself, he'll have pride in a winning Red Sox team. One of my points was, 'You are 1 of 600 of the best in the world at your profession, and if you don't take pride in that, you belong in another job.'

Hope these observations and insights are of some help.

The reader of the above, be he or she a fan, or a player, or a manager present or future, or involved in management, might do well to ponder and retain Mr. Kasko's wise thoughts and observations. The author believes that Eddie, in remarkably effective yet few lines, has summed up the situation past, present, and potential future.

A DOZEN BROTHERLY RED SOX

Sooner or later Boston has had six sets of brothers representing them. Four of these combinations were teammates. Back in 1903, Garland "Jake" Stahl played one game in the outfield when his brother Charles "Chick" Stahl was the distinguished regular center fielder. In 1929, pitcher Milton and catcher Alex Gaston set a precedent for later Red Sox Wes and Rick Ferrell of 1934-1937 fame. Twice, one brother has followed another to Boston, though they did not play at the same time. Catcher John Heving, 1924-1930, was followed by pitcher Joe, 1938-1940, and brotherly outfielders Roy Johnson, 1932-1935, and Bob, 1944-1945, were representatives of that combination. Most recent have been the brothers Conigliaro from Revere, Massachusetts. In 1970, they played alongside in the Red Sox outfield, while at bat they produced a family home run total of 54, which still stands as one of the unique Boston records.

TWO EXAMPLES OF FAITH AND PRIDE: TONY CONIGLIARO AND PUDGE FISK

Tony Conigliaro, after his very serious eye injury late in the 1967 season, never gave up hope and faith, and 3 years later made it back as a Boston regular, being an outfielder again both in 1969 and 1970. After a later stint with California, Tony again tried to make the champion-to-be-Bostons of 1975. He played in only 21 games, hit .123, and failed to stick. But in every other way, Tony C was a success and an inspiration to many, inside and outside of sports. Interviewed by the New York press when the Red Sox made their first visit to Yankee Stadium that year, he was quoted in the *New York Times* issue of April 15, 1975, as follows:

> I pray to the patron saint of miracles, Saint Anthony. I think that in the position I'm in I should explain this to people who need to come back.

GEOGRAPHY, CLIMATE, AND BASEBALL

Everyone realizes that a relationship exists between geography and baseball, including the relatively difficult right-field sunfields in the various parks. On a broader approach, there is a significant relation between state of birth and upbringing of future ball players. To the present time, Red Sox have come from six states in particular: California, Illinois, Massachusetts, New York, Ohio and Pennsylvania. Obviously, California provides much more year-round weather for baseball than do any of the other 5 leading states for future Red Sox. Not in the leaders by numbers is the state of New Hampshire, and catcher Carlton Fisk commented on the subject:

Letter of Carlton Fisk to Clark, February 4, 1974:

> Coming from a baseball-deprived area, New Hampshire, the climate just didn't allow the development of a ball player to take place. . . . coming from Charlestown, N.H., where we played 12 games during the high school season to the Major Leagues and the 162-game schedule is just about the thrill of a lifetime. . . . I was so proud . . . to think a small town boy from Charlestown, N.H. (pop. 1,100), made it to the premiere showcase of Major League baseball.

PHYSICAL HAZARDS OF BOSTON PITCHERS

As has been remarked elsewhere in this volume, Red Sox pitchers as a group have had or are still enjoying exceptionally long lives. The 1911 team is a classic example. Heredity, good health habits, optimistic and active minds, religious faith and a bit of luck appear to be longevity ingredients. The author happened to be the opening speaker at a 1976 BoSox Club luncheon at Anthony's Pier 4 in Boston, and addressed himself to this subject. Manager Paul Richards of the Chicago White Sox followed, remarking, "It's no wonder pitchers live so long as Mr. Clark informs us. They only work every fourth day! It's the managers who go to their graves early!"

Both at and away from the ball park, likely and unlikely accidents and injuries occur. The Boston club has had its unwelcome share of these, including death, over the past 76 seasons. Some examples of ball park incidents include:

1. Joe Wood's falling on wet infield grass and career-end of his pitching.
2. Ty Cobb's bowling over and bloodily spiking Carl Mays as the Detroiter beat out an infield bunt.
3. Babe Ruth's assault on and striking of umpire Brick Owens at Washington, June 23, 1917. Ruth uninjured!
4. Bob Grove and Wes Ferrell, at separate times, kicking and hitting, without injury to themselves, various clubhouse inanimate objects, including water coolers, benches and lockers.
5. The 1947 career-terminating injuries to Hughson and Ferriss.
6. Jose Santiago's damaged arm that failed to respond to surgery.
7. Rick Wise's 1974 arm chill, which ruined his season, in his first game at Fenway, in a cold rain further aggravated by an outdoor TV interview immediately after his victory. Also Jŭan Marichal's multiple physical problems.
8. A Boston sea-gull depositing a fresh fish by the pitcher's mound at Ellis Kinder's feet. Kinder astonished!
9. Jim Pole's fractured-by-line-drive right cheek bone and Luis Tiant's back spasms in 1975.
10. Fergie Jenkins's torn Achilles tendon, while fielding, 1976.

Away from the Park Incidents:

1. 1907 suicide of Manager Chick Stahl.
2. Buck O'Brien assaulted and struck in the eye by irate relative of prominent teammate during 1912 World Series.
3. Babe Ruth's demolishment of an automobile in Boston; Ruth unhurt.
4. Ed Morris's arm injury in a St. Louis elevator.
5. Ed Morris fatally stabbed in Florida fracas, 1932.
6. Jim Lonborg's catastrophic knee injury, Lake Tahoe, 1967.
7. Roger Moret's automobile accident, from which he walked away, 1975.

Other hazards have included blood blisters on pitching fingers, broken fingers and, at least, smarting shins from direct contact with line drives. However, some big-league pitchers truly seemed to have invulnerable bodies for many years: Cy Young, 19 full seasons, including 8 for Boston, and Jack Quinn, 17 full years, 4 and a fraction with the Red Sox.

AILMENTS OF AGE

As ball players grow older, just like other people, the physical shadows of life lengthen. They are subject to the leading killers of Americans, such as cancer (Babe Ruth) and heart failure (Carl Mays). Other diseases, not fatal but very bothersome to those so affected, include crippling arthritis (Ray Collins) and failing eyes (Cy Young). Two distinguished Boston pitchers with whom the author maintained a lively correspondence, George Foster and Carl Mays, each independently advanced the conviction that the protracted strain of pushing their right leg off the pitching rubber eventually caused serious leg problems.

Foster to Clark, March 1, 1955:

I hardly get any place any more. My legs have been pretty bad here [Bokoshe, Oklahoma] all winter. Guess I'm just now beginning to pay for my 20 years in baseball. But for the past week or so I have been walking around pretty good. Took a half mile stroll yesterday and could still make it. Well, bye now, Ellery.

Mays to Clark, January 1, 1970:

I feel fine, but walk with two canes. Guess the old leg that pushed off the rubber all those years feels it has done its duty and wants to call it quits. Thanks again, Ellery, and Happy New Year to you and your family.

1975: A THIRD YAWKEY PENNANT

Table 37

Year	Position	Won	Lost	Net Gain or Loss in Games over Previous Season	ERA	Batting
1974	3 East	84	78	− 5	7(3.72)	4(.264)
1975	1 East	95	65	+12	9(3.98)	1(.275)
1976	3 East	83	79	−13	8(3.52)	5(.263)

The 1975 Red Sox developed a winning recipe and blend of players, with sufficient talent, dedication and consistency, to dethrone Baltimore as East Division champions by 4½ games. Two-thirds of the Boston outfield was represented by sensational rookies Fred Lynn, to be the American League's MVP, and Jim Rice. Together, they batted in 207 runs and either topped or were among the League leaders in six departments:

Doubles	Lynn, first, 47 (highest Red Sox total since Cronin's 51 in 1938)
Slugging Average	Lynn, first, .566
Runs	Lynn, first, 103
Batting	Lynn, second, .331 (highest Red Sox mark since Williams's .388 in 1957)
	Rice, fourth, .309
RBI	Lynn, third, 105
	Rice, fifth, 102

Other Boston offensive leaders included: Cecil Cooper, .333 (36 points higher than his previous club best), Carlton Fisk, .331 (for 79 games after recovering from a spring-training broken arm), and Doyle, .310 (after 8 games for the Angels, he batted 37 points higher than his best previous year). Reminiscent of the early champion Red Sox and indicative of how different men took turns winning games, their RBI leaders, after the first two, were closely bunched: Lynn, 105, Rice, 102 (in game number 144, he suffered a broken arm while batting in Detroit and was out for rest of year), Burleson, 62, Yaz, 60, Petrocelli, 59, Evans, 56, Fisk, 52, and Carbo, 50. As a club the Bostons led the major leagues with a strong .275.

Although their team ERA was not very impressive, it was sufficient. Lee, 17-9, placed fifth in League winning percentage, while the other three of their big 4, Wise, 19-12, Tiant 18-14, and Moret, 14-3, together with Lee, scored 68 wins. Drago and Willoughby contributed valuable saves, with 15 and 8 respectively.

Never off the pace by more than 4 games, on June 29, at Yankee Stadium, where earlier Red Sox teams had had their problems, Moret outpitched Jim "Catfish" Hunter and Boston took the lead never to be headed. Proof of their class was the ability to win on the road (48-31) more than at home (47-34). In close games, those decided by 2 or 1 run, their record was 46-28, and they won two-thirds of their extra-inning contests. A 10-game win streak doubled their longest losing streak of five.

To the victor belongs the various awards: MVP to Lynn; Major League Manager of the Year, Darrell Johnson; Major League Executive of the Year, Vice President Dick O'Connell. But there were clouds on the Boston horizon, though some of the lesser ones disappeared. Fisk recovered from his spring-training fracture, but Rice missed the end of the season, including the playoffs and World Series, because of his fracture of September 21. Moret, the night before he was scheduled to start an important game against the Orioles at Fenway, was involved in a southern New England automobile incident. And Darrell Johnson would not last out the following season, showing how quickly success can be turned around. As usual, Boston fans strongly supported a fine club: 1,748,587, the second highest attendance in club history. The team faced the playoffs for the pennant with desire and confidence against the favored Oakland Athletics, and the Red Sox' estimate of their probable achievement was sustained by the sweep that followed.

1975 CHAMPIONSHIP PLAYOFF

Table 38

Team	Won	Lost	ERA	K	Batting	Runs	RBI	Fielding
Boston	3	0	1.67	14	.316	18	14	.966
Oakland	0	3	4.32	12	.194	7	7	.950

Table 39

LEADING PITCHERS

Name	Won	Lost	IP	ERA	Saves
Tiant	1	0	9	0.00	
Moret	1	0	1	0.00	
Wise	1	0	7⅓	2.45	
Drago	0	0	4⅔	0.00	2

LEADING BATTERS

Name	AB	H	R	RBI	Average
Bando, Oakland	12	6	1	2	.500
Yastrzemski, Boston	11	5	4	2	.455
Burleson, Boston	9	4	2	1	.444
Fisk, Boston	12	5	4	2	.417
Jackson, Oakland	12	5	1	3	.417
Cooper, Boston	10	4	0	1	.400
Lynn, Boston	11	4	1	3	.364

The Red Sox clearly won both the pennant and the statistical playoff. But in the background of the Championship Series, the Athletics had a better regular season than the Red Sox, winning 2 more games and the series between the two, 11 games to 7. Many experts had picked Oakland on this and their previous impressive record of three consecutive World Championships. Some alleged that coach Jimmy Adair, Trainer Joe Romo, whose brother Red is trainer for Joe Duff's U.S. Naval Academy baseball team, and players Sal Bando, Vida Blue, Bert Campaneris, Ken Holtzman, Ted Kubiak, John "Blue Moon" Odom, Joe Rudi, Gene Tenace and Rollie Fingers were beginning to consider the possibility of running out of fingers on which to place their championship rings. But some of these athletes would state after the third game that they had underrated Boston and expected to return home with a split, then win 2 of the next 3 in the best-of-5 series.

Meanwhile, through reliable sources, the Red Sox had been assured that the A's put on their uniforms and spikes in the same way they did and were quite human after all. As a team, Boston was determined and quietly confident.

Ready to take advantage of playing the first two at Fenway, the Bostons zoomed from their dugout, with Luis Tiant on the mound to oppose lefty Ken Holtzman, 18-14, and 2-1 against the Red Sox in the regular season. Pitching at his best, Tiant yielded only 3 hits as his teammates drove Ken out in a 5-run seventh. Exploiting Oakland errors, of which there were 4 of commission, Lynn drove home a pair, with single RBI for Beniquez, Doyle and Burleson. Joe Marcin later commented in his article on the series in *The Official Baseball Guide for 1976:*

> The Boston gardeners, especially Yastrzemski, time and again thwarted A's rallies with great catches and throws, while the A's outfielders behaved, for the most part, as if the whole thing was a strange new experience.

Fielding near Fenway's Green Monster indeed was a problem for the visitors. As one unkind Boston writer observed of left fielder Claudell Washington, "He played his position as if he were dragging a ball and chain."

In the second game, Vida Blue, another lefty, 22-11, and 1-1 against his opponents in the regular campaign, and beaten in three previous World Series appearances, after being staked to an early 3-0 lead over Reggie Cleveland, was torpedoed in the fourth, when Boston rallied to tie. Moret, in relief of Reggie, went on to win with Dick Drago acquiring a save as the Red Sox beat Rollie Fingers, who had been 3-0 against them in the season, by a final margin of 6-3. For the Boston attack, Yaz homered with one on, Petro stroked a solo, Fisk and Lynn added additional single RBI.

With their backs metaphorically to the wall, but pleased to escape from the Green Monster, the A's needed 3 straight at home to pull it out. The Red Sox quickly did them in, for a sweep. Once again starter Holtzman was pounded, leaving in the fifth trailing 3-1. Manager Darrell Johnson took no chances with his starter, Rick Wise, the eventual winner, and put Dick Drago in during the eighth, as he held off the home team, picked up a second save, and the Red Sox won, 5-3. Doyle, Fisk, Petrocelli and Cooper drove in the necessary runs, while Doyle, Yaz, Fisk and Burleson each contributed a pair of hits. The team thoroughly enjoyed their flight back to Boston as the good citizens began their celebrations long before the club's plane touched down at Logan Airport.

1975 WORLD SERIES

Table 40

Team	Won	Lost	ERA	K	Batting	Hits	Runs	RBI	*SB	Fielding
Cincinnati	4	3	3.88	40	.242	59	29	29	9	.993
Boston	3	4	3.86	30	.251	60	30	30	0	.978

*One of these stolen bases developed into an important run, eighth inning of the final game.

Table 41

PITCHING LEADERS

Name and Club	Won	Lost	IP	ERA	Saves	K
Eastwick, Cincinnati	2	0	8	2.25	1	4
Tiant, Boston	2	0	25	3.60		12
Carroll, Cincinnati	1	0	5⅔	3.18		3
Gullett, Cincinnati	1	1	18⅔	4.34		15
McEnaney, Cincinnati	0	0	6⅔	2.70	1	5

Table 42

BATTING LEADERS

Name and Club	AB	BH	R	RBI	Batting
Carbo, Boston	7	3	3	4	.429
Rose, Cincinnati	27	10	3	2	.370
Yastrzemski, Boston	24	9	7	4	.310
Petrocelli, Boston	26	8	3	4	.308
Burleson, Boston	24	7	1	2	.292
Evans, Boston	24	7	3	5	.292
Lynn, Boston	25	7	3	5	.280
Geronimo, Cincinnati	25	7	3	3	.280

As the above stats indicate, the Series was one of the very closest in history. But earlier, before it began, many considered Cincinnati as heavy favorites, due to their wealth of abilities. The Reds finished first in team batting and fielding, third in pitching. Rawley Eastwick chalked up 22 saves, Will McEnaney 15, and 6 pitchers were within the 10-15 victory range: Don Gullett, 15-4, Gary Nolan, 15-9, Jack Billingham, 15-10, Fred Norman, 12-4, Pat Darcy, 11-5, and Clay Kirby, 10-6. Supported by three men in the League's top 15—Joe Morgan, .327, Pete Rose, .317, and Ken Griffey, .305—168 stolen bases in 162 games, and a home record of 64-17, the Reds had raced to a 108-54 record in winning the West Division by 20 games and took the National League pennant in 3 straight from the Pittsburgh Pirates. The Red Sox were not awed by the various media reports.

THE SERIES

First Game: At Boston, Luis Tiant scattered 5 hits in a 6-0 shutout. Boston broke through in the seventh for all their runs. Petrocelli driving in a pair, Yaz, Fisk, Burleson and Cooper each one.

Second Game: Reds evened the Series at Fenway, 3-2. Two Boston base runners tagged out in the opening innings proved costly. Red Sox were ahead, 2-1, when rain delayed the game for 27 minutes in the top half of the seventh. The temperature dropped, and so too did the Red Sox offense. Drago relieved starter Lee after Johnny Bench's double in the ninth. The combination of additional hits by Dave Concepcion and Griffey and Eastwick's two scoreless innings beat the Red Sox.

Third Game: In the first of 3 at Cincinnati, Fisk's solo homer put Boston ahead, but the Reds, scoring 5 runs in 2 innings, drove Wise out. The Red Sox gradually tied the score on Yaz's run in the sixth, Bernie Carbo's pinch 2-run homer in the seventh and Dwight Evans's 2-run clout in the ninth. But the home team won in the bottom of the tenth, 6-5.

With singler Cesar Geronimo on first, pinch bunter Ed Armbrister tried to sacrifice, and according to many, interfered and collided with catcher Fisk; but umpire Barnett made a judgment call that this had not happened. Barnett's decision was significant, as Fisk threw the ball wildly past second trying to get Geronimo, who advanced to third and scored on Morgan's hit.

Fourth Game: Courageous Luis Tiant clung to a Red Sox 5-run advantage gained in the fifth when Evans drove in 2, Burleson, Beniquez and Yaz each one. Good fielding, including Lynn's fine catch in the ninth, and Tiant's determined stamina, evened the Series.

Fifth Game: Reds easily won, 5-2. Gullett prevailed over Reggie Cleveland, who was touched for 2 homers. Eastwick in relief registered a save and the Red Sox were restricted to 5 hits in the game. Yaz and Lynn batted in the visitors' runs.

Sixth Game: One of the most exciting in all Series' history. A dozen pitchers, 8 for Sparky Anderson's Reds, were used in the contest. The Red Sox jumped out in front, 3-0, on Lynn's 3-run homer in first, but Luis Tiant, combed for 11 hits, was removed in the eighth. The three dramatic plays, all by Boston were: Carbo's second pinch homer in bottom of the eighth, scoring Lynn, Petrocelli and himself, evening the game at 6-6; Dewey Evans's preventing a home run by Morgan and turning the catch into a double play in the top of the eleventh; and the most memorable, Carlton Fisk's breaking up the game as first man up for Boston in the eleventh, driving the ball against and off the left-field foul pole for a home run. Leaping and applauding his efforts, Carlton was joined by teammates and fans as the Red Sox for a second time had tied the Series.

Seventh Game: Many Red Sox, including Captain Carl, hoped and even expected their momentum would carry them on to victory the next day, but it was not to be. After Gullett yielded 4 walks and the Red Sox made a pair of hits, for 3 runs in the third, Boston bats grew cold and they scored no more runs. Meanwhile, the Reds pecked away at Bill Lee; Perez's 2-run homer in sixth got them close. After Griffey walked in the seventh, reliever Moret yielded a run-scoring single and it was tied.

Rookie Jim Burton was Manager Johnson's selection to pitch the ninth, later providing second-guessers a conversation piece.

Griffey walked, advanced to third via a sacrifice and fielder's choice, then scored the decisive run on Morgan's short single to center. In the final 4 innings, Boston had not been able to get a hit off Billingham, Clay Carroll or McEnaney..

Commentary on the 1975 World Series: Millions of Americans had been thrilled with the great effort of the Red Sox as TV watchers broke all existing records, according to media estimates. Boston individual players, combining both their percentage of League Championship Series and World Series receipts, received individual checks of $13,325.87, an interesting amount when compared with the Red Sox' all-time lowest individual checks of $890.00 to each member of their 1918 World Champions. But perhaps a dollar went 15 times as far in those earlier years.

With both short- and long-term perspectives, the 1975 Red Sox reviewed the situation. For the third time in Mr. Yawkey's years of ownership, the team had gone down fighting in a World Series, carrying each one to the full limit of 7 games. Of course, they had every right to feel disappointed after such a magnificent attempt, but proud of their overall performance from early April through October 22. The breaks had gone against them, such as the rain delay in the second contest, at Boston, during which seemingly the Boston offense had cooled while that of the visitors had improved. If the rain had continued and the game been called, a Red Sox victory would have resulted. But the events were otherwise. In the third game, at Cincinnati's Riverfront Stadium, umpire Barnett's controversial call had seriously affected the game's outcome. However, official results are just that.

The next summer, on the afternoon of July 9, Vice President Dick O'Connell announced to a hushed group of Boston Red Sox players the death of Thomas A. Yawkey. It appears almost a certainty that every one present at that time who had been on the 1975 Champions felt even more keenly than during the previous fall the loss to Cincinnati, because Mr. Yawkey now had gone to his reward and the teams of 1946, 1967 and 1975, though all making splendid efforts, had not quite been able to win for him that most cherished title in American professional baseball. But Mr. Yawkey, a very outstanding sportsman, in his own disappointments was too much of a fine man and philosopher to place the results over and above how his team had played the game, to the best of their abilities, in each of those final Series.

The excitement and drama of the 1975 World Series was a fitting epitaph for Mr. Yawkey. One of Yawkey's charges, Rick Burleson, has this to say about the Series:

Burleson to Clark, March 19, 1977:

> To this point in my Red Sox career, I have several great memories. One was Yaz's great all-around play against Oakland which helped us get into the World Series. Others were my making three hits in the first Series' game and Carlton Fisk's winning home run in the sixth contest. And earlier, Fred Lynn's 10 RBIs in Detroit. 1975 was a great year!

1976

Almost simultaneous with Yaz's flyout to left center that ended the 1975 World Series, a wave of what turned out to be unfounded optimism and confidence engulfed many Red Sox fans and players. Expectations that the team next year would obtain its two just rewards, both titles, were enhanced additionally by the off-season acquisition of Fergie Jenkins, a 7-time 20-game winner. At spring training, the overconfident team and its fans believed what they heard, said and read. Nevada-based professional gamblers established the club as first choice in the division.

Ten months later, on January 27, 1977, as reported in the next-day issue of the *Boston Herald Advertiser,* Captain Yastrzemski confided to listeners at the 38th Annual Boston Baseball Writers' Dinner:

> One thing we can't do is be overconfident as we were last year. We thought all we had to do was to throw our gloves on the field and we would win. It doesn't work that way in baseball. . . . talent is no good unless all 25 pull together.

By May, 1976, the club hit an iceberg of 10-straight defeats that crushed its spirit and hopes. Reliever Jim Willoughby, in the October 23, 1976, issue of the *Sporting News,* was quoted as having reflected of this incident:

> I think you can learn a lot from a season like this. Boston has some players who never experienced a losing season. They had no idea how to react, and there is no question in my mind that the 10 games in a row we lost in early May decided the whole season for us.

Compounding mounting Red Sox problems, Bill Lee was severely injured when he participated in an early-season Yankee Stadium Brawl, while at the other end of the campaign, Jenkins, who had a tendency to weaken in late innings, tore his right-foot Achilles tendon in a fielding play and missed the remainder of the season. Personnel strain and tension additionally was increased by protracted salary-contract negotiations involving Lynn, Fisk and Burleson, reportedly upsetting some others who had signed theirs before the official season began.

Before the July 19 dismissal of Darrell Johnson, on June 15, in Oakland, where the Red Sox were on a road trip, and 6 games off the pace, came startling and pleasing news to Boston fans. Charley Finley announced the sales of Rollie Fingers and Joe Rudi to Boston, and that of Vida Blue to the Yankees.

One very strange event happened during the summer of 1976, and this was Commissioner Kuhn's voiding the June 15 sale by Charlie Finley of Rollie Fingers and Joe Rudi to the Red Sox and Vida Blue to the Yankees. Rollie and Joe were with Boston long enough to suit up, get their pictures taken and have many fans speculate what they might have done for the club if the sales had been declared in the best interests of baseball by Mr. Kuhn, thereby making them legal. He decided otherwise.

Kuhn's decision recently was upheld by a U.S. District Court Judge. Meanwhile, the Red Sox added Bob Campbell during the 1976 off-season to bolster their bullpen, and the pleasing settlement of Luis Tiant's contract dispute made the Red Sox, on the

eve of the 1977 pennant race, the major threat to the American
League champion Yankees. One heartening development for the
Bostons and their fans was the announced determination of the
team to atone for 1976 and the quiet confidence that the Red
Sox, in recent years very difficult to predict, will do their best
to live up to their desire. Thus, once again, intangibles appear
to be very influential in the history of the Boston club. For those
who believe in the influence of previous history, one hundred
years ago, led by Tommy Bond, born in Ireland and with a 40-17
record, the Boston Red Stockings won the National League pennant, winning 42 of their 60 games.

Yet, in 1976, manager Darrell Johnson was unable to lift the
club through and above a mine field of obstacles; tempers grew
short, and near the end of the season, Johnson was relieved of
his duties. Coach Don Zimmer, well-liked and respected by the
players, was appointed on July 19. On the last day, aided by the
rain-out of Cleveland's final games, the club raised itself to a
modest third, 15½ games behind the champion Yankees, who had
started fast and run away with the pennant, followed by the
Orioles, 10½ lengths behind.

Turnabouts in seasonal performance were numerous. Whereas
the big pitching 4 of 1975 had posted 76 victories, Tiant, Wise,
Jenkins and Cleveland, their most productive moundsmen in
1976, gained only 57. Only Luis Tiant, 21-12, and second in
League wins, had an outstanding season. Jim Willoughby was
best in club ERA at 2.82 but had a 3-12 record because of the
team's failure to get him runs while he was their reliever.

In batting, the Red Sox as a team were down some 12 points
from 1975. Both Lynn and Rice did not match their spectacular
freshman years. But they did well, Fred placing second in
slugging average, while Jim was fourth and also tied for fourth
in home runs. Whereas the club's 6 leading RBI men in 1975 had
totaled 444, the 1976 group scored 450; but it appears that these
were less timely delivered than those of 1975 in scoring critical
runs during close games. Comparing RBI of continuing Bostons
in these 2 seasons, Lynn was down 40, Petrocelli, no longer a
regular, 35 fewer, Rice, off 17, and Doyle, 10. On the improved

side, Yaz had a gain of 42 for a season's total of 102, Cooper was up 34, Burleson, 20, Fisk and Evans, each 6. Dewey Evans, in addition to placing second (tie) for League doubles' leadership, topped all outfielders in fielding .994, with only 2 errors in 341 chances. Lynn was the club's top hitter, with .314.

Between seasons, ticket promotion was most successful and attendance rose to 1,895,846; highest since 1968, and this marked the tenth consecutive season over a million. The team for the thirty-first consecutive year smashed over 100 home runs, 134, to extend their already-held League consecutive achievement record, Yaz also increased his all-time Red Sox leaderships in games and at bats.

CARL YASTRZEMSKI (1961-present)

Carl, now beginning his seventeenth season for the Red Sox, is second in longevity only to Ted Williams and, of course, is the greatest Boston batter still in service. Yaz, dividing his time between the outfield and first base, has been a brilliant fielder in left, a capable first baseman, and, in recent years, captain of the team, setting a remarkably fine personal example in troubled 1976. Each game he plays and each new at bat finds him further extending his record as All-time Boston leader in those categories. In addition, he has been a League seasonal leader over 20 times to date. Here are some excerpts from his remarkable career:

Table 43

AMERICAN LEAGUE SEASONAL LEADERSHIP IN SELECTED CATEGORIES

Category	Leader in Year(s)				
Most Valuable Player	1967				
Outfield Assists	1962,	1963,	1964,	1969,	1971
Batting	1963,	1967,	1968		
Runs	1967,	1970,	1974		
Hits	1963,	1966			
Total Bases	1967,	1970			
Walks	1963,	1968			
Doubles	1963,	1966			
Home Runs	1967 (tie)				
RBI	1967				

Table 44

BOSTON ALL-TIME CAREER BATTING

Category	Position	Achievement
Games	1	2,421
At Bats	1	8,848
Hits	2	2,559
Runs	2	1,402
RBI	2	1,343
Doubles	2	489
Home Runs	2	338
Extra Base Hits	2	877
Total Bases	2	4,162
Slugging Average	9	.470

1976 was somewhat of a banner year for Yaz, but the year would be most remembered for a very, very sad event—the passing of Thomas A. Yawkey, on July 9.

THOMAS A. YAWKEY, PRESIDENT OF THE BOSTON AMERICAN LEAGUE BASEBALL CLUB, 1933-1976

During the 44 years of Mr. Yawkey's distinguished association with the city of Boston, its fans and ball club, he contributed to the happiness and welfare of many people in many ways. In the special area of professional baseball, he stood out as a fine sportsman, able to gain satisfaction for the several good efforts some of his teams made and not to show disappointment that three pennants, rather than more, and no World Championships, instead of at least one, had been gained. He was man enough to take all this in full and graceful Yawkey stride, congratulating the winners and not harboring bitterness or remorse because limited success had been his portion.

To this author, and increasingly so as Mr. Yawkey grew older, the owner projected a fatherly image of a gentleman dedicated, sincere, modest, and paternally interested in the lives and problems of every one who worked for him or who in some way was connected with baseball. A people's man, thoroughly and deservedly loved by hundreds of ball players and thousands of other persons inside and outside the Boston organization, the

TED WILLIAMS. No one man, other than possibly Babe Ruth or Tris Speaker, probably will ever come into discussion more when fans explore the subject, "The Red Sox' Greatest Batter." To date, he has been the most controversial, publicized and unfortunately criticized Red Sox player in history. There is at least one significant mutual characteristic between Ted and "the greatest owner in the American League," the late Tom Yawkey. Each shared a compassion for people, each avoided publicity in this respect. Ted's off-the-field concern for the many poor children afflicted with deadly cancer was enduringly shown by his many visits to hospitals and his abilities to raise monies for the continued research and facilities of The Jimmy Fund. Boston's greatest batter holds the team's all-time leadership in 9 categories, with Yaz in recent years having taken over 2 others that he formerly held. (*Courtesy of the Boston Red Sox*)

CARL YASTRZEMSKI. Undoubtedly the greatest living active Red Sox player, endurance and ability are two of his benchmarks. The captain of the team and a man who should be an inspiration to his many younger teammates, Yaz often has unfairly been the recipient of the fickleness of a small proportion of Fenway's audiences. Every time he steps out on the field, every time he stands in the Boston batter's box, new records are created, reminding many faithful and loyal Red Sox fans that they are continuing to have the privilege of seeing one of their greatest all-time athletes in action. (*Courtesy of Bill Clark*)

February 1, 1977

Dear Ellery,

Sorry for the delay in answering your letter, but your request has been difficult for me to put into words.

When I took the job managing the Red Sox in 1970, I felt the only way to win and accomplish the job for the Red Sox was to try to maintain a dedicated attitude by each and every player. They had to act as a single solid unit. This was harder to accomplish as the years went on, and I imagine it is a near impossible task today.

Let me preface my observations by remembering the player-manager relationship when I was a player. Then the manager almost had dictatorial powers. What he said was law. The prime reason being fear. Fear of losing a starting job, fear of fines, or fear of being sent to the minors. The manager had a "hammer".

I felt a change taking place when I started managing. There was more managing "off the field" in order to maintain a feeling of spirit and unity on the field. Today, as I said before, it must be a near impossible task.

-2-

Blame it on a looser society, higher salaries, or fewer minor leagues, a situation that forces players into the major leagues at an earlier age with less experience, or something else. The fact is, attitudes have changed. The weapons in a manager's arsenal are slowly disappearing. Fines wind up as a grievance before the player's association, demotion to the minor leagues is out of the question for various reasons, and benching a regular as a form of dicipline is out of the question. Player contracts as a whole are longer and for more money than a manager's, which creates a difficult situation.

My approach to managing the Red Sox was to try to bring out the personal pride in each player. If a player has pride in himself, he'll have pride in a winning Red Sox team. One of my points was, "You are 1 of 600 of the best in the world at your profession, and if you don't take pride in that, you belong in another job".

Hope these observations and insights are of some help.

Sincerely yours,

Eddie Kasko

TIMELY WORDS BY EDDIE KASKO. This letter is highly recommended reading for all managers and ball players, contemporary, prospective and retired. The perceptive, gentlemanly Eddie Kasko has said it all in a few very well considered and expressed words as he most kindly reviewed some of the duties, recent problems and challenges of a major-league manager. Boston is indeed fortunate to have their former manager (1970-1973) currently serving as a scout and sharing his many attributes on behalf of the team and its future players.

"OH, SAY, CAN YOU SEE?" Mention of the annual *Red Sox Press-TV-Radio Guide* instantly brings thoughts of their producer, Bill Crowley, Director of Public Relations. This valuable, compact guide is only a part of the continuing evidence of Bill's multi-faceted services to the Boston club, and proof of the old saying, "The effectiveness of any organization largely is dependent upon that of its dedicated staff." Increasingly, avid baseball memorabilia collectors treasure such outstanding brochures as these, which summarize and statistically tabulate important tangibles of Red Sox 76-year history. (*Courtesy of the Boston Red Sox*)

BERNIE CARBO. To the delight of thousands of Red Sox fans, Bernie, last fall, returned to Boston, following his brief departure after having made a pleasant entry into Mr. Spink's *Official World Series Records*. Two Series pinch-hit home runs not only kept Boston's 1975 hopes alive, but proved that Carbo is a man who mastered tension and could deliver when the pressure was on—the Red Sox were trailing in both those games. The hopes of Boston for 1977 will in part rest on Bernie's abilities again to thrust the club into a forward position. (*Courtesy of the Boston Red Sox*)

RICK BURLESON. Although the current Red Sox second-base strength appears uncertain, at shortstop, Rick has been a tower of mobile power with his very strong arm and good ground coverage. Rick was one of the many keys to the 1975 pennant. Last year some fans believed that his extended contract negotiations might have been detrimental to his playing. Whether unrelated or not, after the salary arrangements were effected, his late-season play was very good. His nickname of "the rooster" may indicate to some of the optimistic fans early sounds of possible victory in 1977. (*Courtesy of the Boston Red Sox*)

DWIGHT EVANS. "Dewey" appears to have won the right field position on the team, possibly to produce over a period of years with defensive abilities comparable to those of Harry Hooper. Certainly his catch off Joe Morgan in the eleventh inning of the sixth 1975 Series game, and his brilliance in leading all American League outfielders in 1976 with a sparkling .994 lends credence to such a comparison. Personal improvement at the bat probably will be made as Manager Zimmer eyes a very promising outfield in 1977. (*Courtesy of the Boston Red Sox*)

REGGIE CLEVELAND. 1977 may well prove to be a turning point in both Red Sox and Reggie Cleveland history. Manager Zimmer is very much impressed with the tangible and intangible improvements in Reggie's pitching. His willpower, determination and increased ERA effectiveness, provide foundations for optimism. Last season, he finished fourteenth in League ERA effectiveness, the highest position for a Red Sox pitcher, except for Luis Tiant, since Bill Lee's third position in 1973. (*Courtesy of the Boston Red Sox*)

JIM RICE. Jim can also assign season 1976 somewhat to the category of learning and accumulated wisdom. With a great rookie year overshadowed only by his teammate Fred Lynn, Rice was dealt an unexpected 1975 reversal. His late season injury kept him out of the American League Playoff and the World Series. It is not idle speculation that the hotly contested series would have been influenced by Jim's outstanding bat. Many baseball authorities believe that Jim has outstanding potential. Lynn and Rice finished 2-4 in League slugging percentage last season. (*Courtesy of the Boston Red Sox*)

FRED LYNN. Now at the start of his th Boston season, Fred well knows the impli tions of the so-called sophomore jinx, frequently written about by natio sports writers. The outstanding rookie Red Sox history to date, he deservedly v the various American League tang accolades of 1975. Season 1976 still wa good one, although some fans expected much too soon from Fred. The real test his great abilities will come in 1977, and the positive side, the settlement, last seas of his salary disputes may well help insure his full concentration on the ga this season. (*Courtesy of the Boston F Sox*)

LUIS TIANT. The greatest active Red Sox pitcher, Luis is about to become only the sixth Red Sox pitcher in 77 years to win 100 or more games. Currently, he has 97 victories. Perhaps the most amazing feature of the achievement is that only Luis Tiant and the Red Sox management of 1971 had the faith and confidence to believe that he was not all done as a pitcher. The facts have spoken for themselves. The most popular member of the club, its constant and ready wit, Tiant has won the hearts of thousands, perhaps millions, of Boston fans. Babe Ruth may have prospered years ago, in part, on his famous cigar that bore his name; but Luis and his much more famous favorite smoke has brought many pleasant moments to Boston baseball. (*Courtesy of the Boston Red Sox*)

RICK WISE. Although Boston has two prospectively effective rookie mounds men, 1977 pitching probably will de pend more on their veterans, of whom Rick Wise is very important. His 1974 arm chill, during and after a nationally televised early season game in Boston limited his seasonal pitching to only 49 innings. Recovered in 1975, he topped the championship team's pitchers with 19 victories but, in 1976, in common with many other teammates, did no have nearly as effective a season. A veteran, intelligent, and dedicated bal player, Wise doubtless is pointing to ward 1977 with a determined finger Among his probable hopes is the wearing of a World Series championship ring which would be the first one on any Red Sox finger in 59 years. (*Courtesy of the Boston Red Sox*)

OLDEST LIVING RED SOX FAN! Herbert "Dad" Gallagher celebrated his 102nd birthday in July, 1976, by attending the special luncheon given by Northeastern University at the opening of Ellery Clark's Boston Bicentennial Exhibit on "The Early Red Sox: The Huntington Avenue Grounds Era of 1901-1911." It was most appropriate to honor this oldest known Red Sox fan, and Mr. Gallagher thrilled the receptive audience after the festivities by demonstrating exactly how he held and threw his curve ball of some 84 years ago. Mr. Gallagher, earlier a representative for a Boston area lumber firm, recalled how he kept his sales visits within a restricted radius of the ball park when it was known and advertised ahead of time that Cy Young was to pitch. Left to right: author, Jack Grinold, Northeastern University's Director of Sports Information, and Herbert "Dad" Gallagher. (*Courtesy of Northeastern University*)

"MR. RED SOX"—THE LATE TOM YAWKEY. President Thomas A. Yawkey and Vice President and General Manager Richard H. O'Connell are book recipients during Boston's great 1975 season. Few, if any, realized at that time, or during the above-photographed pleasant moment, that this would be the last full year of Mr. Yawkey's distinguished life. It is most fitting to conclude the pictorial section of this volume with the many thoughts and emotions Mr. Yawkey's beloved memory brings to millions of Americans, especially those who are also dedicated to the Boston Red Sox cause. (*Courtesy of the Boston Red Sox*)

full, sustained sunshine of his character and influence was felt by grateful Americans. He did not hold grudges and, for example, made his peace with Dick Williams some time before his death.

Critics have attacked Mr. Yawkey, claiming the "Gold Sox" were a country club of spoiled stars, privileged players who would be condoned and supported by him, if the matter got that far, in incidents involving the players and their manager. The author believes Mr. Yawkey regarded his associates as members of his family and in his continuing boyish enthusiasm greatly enjoyed the personal friendships and conversations with a number of his very prominent players, such as Ted Williams and Carl Yastrzemski. Certain Red Sox players who may not have done their all-around best for Mr. Yawkey and the team, on and off the field, have very good reason, should they be that retrospective, to feel genuinely sorry, even at this late date, that they disappointed both themselves and the team, of which Mr. Yawkey was the overall symbol.

The head of the Boston Red Sox family physically has left us, but never in spirit, dedication, kindness, faith, understanding of human frailties and fondness for those with whom he came in contact. No World Championship flag ever flew from his center-field flagpole, but in the appreciative mind's eye of millions of Americans and fine Boston fans, an intangible pennant forever will wave from Fenway in honor of his memory and lasting contributions to the game, to Boston, and to all those associated with the team directly or indirectly. Ted Williams said it all in a very few words in a December 29, 1976, letter to the author:

> Certainly last year was a very sad one for all Red Sox fans when Mr. Yawkey, the greatest president of a major league team, passed away.

CONCLUSIONS

1. Boston baseball team success is a difficult blend, probably in about equal proportions, of the intangible and tangible qualities already identified and discussed. Unfortunately, unlike the famous *Boston Cooking School Book* of decades ago, it cannot be printed as a sure success recipe. If and when a Red Sox team has been able to put it all together, as they have done on nine occasions to date, only twice have they been able to maintain this blend for two consecutive seasons. There are so many variables in personalities and situations that continuation of the successful blend is very tenuous.

2. Ideally, the Red Sox manager should be an effective, discerning leader, dedicated to the best team effort and achievement possible, skilled in getting the most out of his men, able to gain and maintain their individual and group respect and support. He must realize there are as many different personalities as there are team members, and that all, if they will produce their full share of cooperation, should be devoted to the team's success above all else. The manager, since the statistics show he spends only a little over two years in Boston, must realize that time is short and the challenge great. He should be at least as proficient in practical psychology—and he does not need a college degree as a qualification—as he is in the mechanics of baseball.

3. The players' intangible qualities should include desire, dedication, pride, unity, at least reasonable confidence, consistency of positive attitude, and the ability to produce under stress and strain and to handle with grace and skill unexpected adverse situations. Their most important single intangible asset is contained in seven words—*the success of*

the Red Sox team. Their necessary tangibles should include good physical health, strength, endurance, consistency and close to full capacity in the various well-known offensive and defensive categories by which ball players are judged (and sometimes over-judged to the exclusion of the intangibles). Contracts reflect RBIs, home runs, ERAs and won-lost records rather than the intangible assets.

4. Owners, general managers, directors, managers, coaches and players should study, even if belatedly, and recognize the available, enduring lessons of previous Boston team failure and success and apply these findings to the improvement of the club. In American baseball in general, there are too many limited students of the game, and an overexposure of the mechanics of pitching, batting, base running and fielding. Too few students regard the author's central theme— the *equal* significance of intangibles *and* tangibles. Quite possibly, baseball men, as in most other professions, are too prone to leave unexamined the available practical, constructive examples from the experiences of their predecessors, naïvely choosing instead to try to do it all on their own without useful recourse to the sweat, tears and some smiles of their predecessor losers and winners.

5. As this book has tried to prove, pitching ability, including depth of the staff, and timely RBI power, appear to be the most frequent characteristics of championship teams, Boston or otherwise. However, 1967 was an exception, as noted. The 76-year Red Sox profile to date reveals above average batting, below average pitching, and weak base stealing.

6. As in warfare, actual or potential, an intelligent baseball team never should underestimate another team's potential. It can be fatal to assume that a team of one season will be a carbon-copy of the previous season's team. The Yankees of 1976 were quite different from those of 1975. Championships are won and lost both on and off the field, on a 24-hour, day-by-day basis; success is not soley determined by the hours spent actually in uniform. The Red Sox of 1967 were a splendid example of this truth.

7. Sustained injuries to key personnel, such as those that happened to the 1913, 1947 and 1968 Red Sox, can be disastrous, especially if the bench is not deep and if satisfactory replacements are not available on short order. Obviously, both the club physician and trainer are of great importance.

8. Ball players should not regard what is in print as being of eternal and uncontrovertible truth, with the exception of the generally very accurate statistics officially compiled at the end of each season. Overly optimistic articles of conjecture, predicting certain success on the basis of immediate past records, can be proven wrong, as the 1976 Red Sox discovered. Pennants are won not in November nor in January, but championship steps are taken as early as March, when there are certain signs of winning, perhaps difficult to discover in the generally relaxed atmosphere of spring training; but most of the preseason optimism is related to the intangibles rather than the tangibles. Many a blazing fast ball or wicked curve or robust hit have been left behind when the teams make their annual return to their home city.

9. However great a club may be in the intangibles, unless there is also relative competence in the tangibles, no pennant flag will wave in the breeze. There is no known satisfactory substitute either for knowledge or for competent ball players. But if the race is close and the ability of contending teams is about equal, then superiority in the intangibles will carry the day. Boston proved it in 1967.

10. From reading the seventy selected personal letters written to the author the past 50 years by prominent Red Sox, it is obvious that many of the players had or have very perceptive, inquiring minds, often thinking beyond the mere scope of technical baseball. Among the baseball set, and definitely held in great respect by his teammates, pitcher Bill Lee's vast fund of knowledge and philosophy have added much to the overall image of the club. The following 1977 letter from Bill Lee is an excellent example:

I'm not really qualified to speak on many subjects, but here goes. Life is going too fast and baseball is trying to catch up with it. But people love baseball because it's a slow pace pastorial [*sic*] game. But now we're getting DHs and astroturf and playing in stadiums instead of parks. We used to take pride in fundamentals. Now we love speed and artificial substances like our food.

I don't like baseball, it's getting so specialized, because every race that becomes specialized also becomes *extinct*. The whales will die in my son's lifetime and I'm sad. Slow down baseball, get into harmony with natural systems.

They call me the spaceman but all I'm trying to do is save the earth.

11. Of course, many baseball men are religiously minded, but Luis Tiant is one who fully appreciates the joys of family fellowship so long denied his devoted family. Separated from his parents for so many years, Luis never gave up the hope of seeing them again. Late in August, 1975, Luis Tiant's parents arived in Boston from their native Cuba. It was the first time Luis had seen his father in 15 years; the first time he had seen his mother in eight years. The elder Tiant, generally regarded as the finest pitcher in Cuba's history, had never seen his son play in the major leagues. Boston went on to win the AL East title six weeks later, then beat Oakland for the AL pennant. On October 4th, Luis' parents were part of the capacity crowd which saw him shut out the mighty Reds, 6-0, in the World Series opener at Fenway Park. The following is Luis Tiant's, "My Favorite Memory in Baseball," from his dramatic biography, *El Tiante*, published by Doubleday in 1976:

I had some company over to my house the night before the first game of the 1975 World Series, and I didn't get to bed until 2 a.m. But I slept like a baby.

Before I went to sleep, though, I lay there relishing the good memories—the 20-game seasons, the friends I'd made—but this club, this season, this time, was the sweetest of all. I thought, "How lucky I am—my world is finally all coming together. We'd had a good season; we'd knocked off the A's and made it to the World Series, the big dream for any ballplayer."

I lay there thinking about all of the things that had happened to me: the years in Cleveland when I pitched good, but the team was never good enough to win; the time I hurt my arm in Minnesota and they cut me; all of the years when Maria and the kids lived in Mexico City and we couldn't be together; and all of the years I couldn't see my parents.

Of all the hurts, the separation from my parents was the worst. We think we have so many problems as we go through life, but then some *real* problems come along and we start to realize that all of the other ones just weren't that important. Family problems can hurt so much. Like seeing your child ill and not being able to do anything about it. Or watching your father die and not being able to stop it. I see my fellow Cubans in this country and I watch them suffer because of the things that are happening back home, and I suffer with them. I know of some whose parents have died, and they couldn't even go home to bury them. That's not right. Those problems hurt so badly.

So many times I'd think about my father dying before we could see each other again. I tried not to think those things, but I couldn't help it. He was getting old and he was still going to work every day, pumping gas at a garage, and I couldn't even send him a dime for a cup of coffee. Nothing. I wasn't allowed to do anything to make life easier for my parents. There were times I'd think about them and I'd start to cry. There are no two people in the world like your parents. No one else loves you like they do. I was their only child, and I couldn't do anything for them.

All those old thoughts were in my mind that night as I lay there.

I was in my own home. I had Maria and our children with me. I had my parents with me. I had so many good friends. And I had my career. There were so many years when I had none of those, when everything seemed to be wrong.

Now everything was right. There was no more I could ask for. When I wake up in the morning, we'd all go to the park and I'd pitch in the World Series, something I had waited all my life to do. And best of all, my parents were here to share it with me.

I closed my eyes and said a little prayer. I thanked God for making all these things happen, and especially for bringing my parents and me together again.

In all the years I've been playing baseball, I have never been as happy as I was that night. It was like all of my prayers had been answered at once.

So I said, "Thank you, God," and sleep came.

Tiant's father died on December 10, 1976. His mother died two nights later, and they were buried a few miles from Luis's home in a joint service.

12. With these philosophies and conclusions in mind, the author appends two carefully selected quotations with which to end this chapter. Although some readers will criticize these selections as no longer being possible or applicable, the author gives them his full support, believing them to be in perfect accord with his optimistic philosophy of Boston Red Sox baseball, past, present and future.

1964 Letter of Harry Hooper to Clark:

> From 1909 through 1918 I never got over $10,000—average about $6,500. . . . We played for the honor of winning. As Larry Gardner said, 'We had fun.' We had to have fun because we didn't get much money. I always felt I would rather win and get the loser's share than lose and get the winner's share.

From *1919 Reach's Official American League BaseBall Guide* (Excerpt from George Whiteman's interview, following his selection as Hero of the 1918 World Series. George, after years in the minors, finally was signed by the 1918 Red Sox to play left and bat fourth when Ruth pitched):

> They all want to talk to me now. . . . It came late, but I got my chance at last. I was sure I could make good and I guess I have. . . . I had been on pennant-winning teams several times in the minors. . . . I went plodding along year after year, hoping that something would break. I had about given up hope when this chance came, and I said to myself: 'It's the last chance you will get and it is up to you to make good.' I worked hard all the time. I did my best.

BOSTON BASEBALL LONGEVITY

Longevity is a subject of obvious continuing interest to people of all generations and nationalities. The longevity record of early Boston Red Sox baseball teams (1901-1911) is an important but hitherto unexamined subject. Now that the life span of almost all of these pre-Fenway Park players is over, it is time to examine the facts and draw inferences and conclusions.

Longevity and Boston baseball have been associates for many years. George Wright, who played shortstop on the original Boston Red Stockings of 1871 and helped bring to the city the first 6 of an eventual 23 championships to date, lived to be 90. In 1925, when Mr. Wright encouraged the author, then a young Boston boy, to write about Boston baseball, neither one anticipated that one of its aspects, longevity, would be evaluated some 52 years later.

The average life span of Red Sox regulars and near-regulars of 1901-1911 was 70.4 years, with three still alive in 1977. The Huntington Avenue Grounds Era (1901-1911) spawned an unusual, paradoxical club in 1906. Not only by coincidence was it the median year at the original ball field, but the 1906 team, undaunted by the club's worst seasonal performance (49-105), eventually set the highest longevity average—74.6 years. The median year of birth for club members of that year was 1876, when, according to the best available calculations, the expected life span of an American male baby was only 41.4 years. Since the members of the early Boston Americans exceeded the mean life span by the average of 29 years, the subject deserves examination and comment. First, the statistics—team and individual:

Table 45

EARLY RED SOX TEAM LONGEVITY STATISTICS

Team of Season	Group Longevity
1901	68.0
1902	70.8
1903	70.2
1904	71.4
1905	74.5
1906	74.6
1907	71.2
1908	66.1
1909	67.4
1910	69.6
1911	70.7
	Average 70.4

Table 46

LONGEVITY OF 34 PROMINENT SENIOR FORMER MEMBERS

1901-1911 BOSTON RED SOX

Name	Position	Boston Years	Age
Fred Parent	Infield	1901-1907	96
Fred Mitchell	Pitcher	1901-1902	92
Walter Nagle	Pitcher	1911	91
Larry Gardner	Infield	1908-1917	89
Cy Young	Pitcher	1901-1908	88
Nick Altrock	Pitcher	1902-1903	88
Duffy Lewis	Outfield	1910-1917	89*
Marty McHale	Pitcher	1910-1911	88*
Harry Hooper	Outfield	1909-1920	87
Ralph Glaze	Pitcher	1906-1908	87
Joe Wood	Pitcher	1908-1915	87*
Harry Gleason	Infield-Outfield	1901-1903	86
Joe Riggert	Outfield	1911	86
Hyland Gunning	Infielder	1911	86
Bill Carrigan	Catcher	1906-1916	85
Harry Wolter	Infield-Outfield-Pitcher	1909	85
Tracy Baker	Infielder	1911	85
Eddie Cicotte	Pitcher	1908-1912	84
Joe Harris	Pitcher	1905-1907	84
Jesse Burkett	Outfield	1905	84
Jacob Volz	Pitcher	1901	84
Kip Selbach	Outfield	1904-1906	83
Harry Morgan	Pitcher	1907-1909	83
Al Shaw	Catcher	1909	83
Frank Barberich	Pitcher	1910	83

Table 46 (continued)

Name	Position	Boston Years	Age
Ray Collins	Pitcher	1909-1915	82
Norwood Gibson	Pitcher	1903-1906	82
Jesse Tannehill	Pitcher	1904-1908	82
Steve Yerkes	Infield	1909-1914	82
Gabby Cravath	Outfield	1908	82
Elmer Steele	Pitcher	1907-1909	81
John Killilay	Pitcher	1911	81
Pat Donahue	Catcher	1908-1910	81
John Knight	Infield	1907	80

*Denotes alive In 1977

The names in the above list range from brilliant, long-tenured Hall of Famers, among them Cy Young and Harry Hooper, to such outstanding players as Parent, Wood, Lewis, Gardner and Carrigan, to others just a notch or two below, and finally to a relatively obscure few. Volz and Barberich were two in this latter category; they pitched between them only about 12 innings for the early Red Sox. Baker played one game for the 1911 team. But whether passing through Boston for a few cups of coffee and a plate of famous baked beans, or there for an athletic lifetime, or perhaps somewhere in between, the entire group eventually had one common but uncommon bond—a life span some 29 years beyond average.

Undoubtedly, there is a correlation between the author's research on player-selected great Boston memories and the current study. For example, on pages 27-28 of his *Boston Red Sox: 75th Anniversary History, 1901-1975,* he noted the prevalence of pitchers among the total of 40 respondents to his questionnaires of 1930-1974. By position, the percentiles of respondents were:

Pitchers	42.4%
Infielders	26.3%
Outfielders	23.8%
Catchers	7.5%

Of course, catchers, numerically, were obvious minorities in comparison with the other groups.

An analysis of the 34 most senior former **Red Sox**, according to baseball position, provides these percentiles:

Pitchers	50.9%
Outfielders	20.1%
Infielders	20.1%
Catchers	8.9%

Thus, the prominence of pitchers in both tables and analyses indicates that they were and are a hardy breed, enjoyed cooperating with at least one research-minded fan, and generally possessed to the end of their lives excellent mental capacities, including good memory and the desire and ability to communicate well. All these factors, of course, are conducive to long and useful lives. It appears evident that most pitchers realize the exceptional physical and mental demands placed upon them early in their athletic lives; therefore, they readily understand the necessity of keeping in as good a condition as possible. Continuing emphasis on good condition in later years quite naturally occurs, and such was the case with Boston's moundsmen.

Clearly, the percentiles on outfielders and infielders are too close to permit discernment between them. However, on the controversial subject of the best outfield or outfields in the period 1880-1922, longevity statistics markedly favor the Boston Americans, also the Boston Nationals, over others. Boston fans still consider Lewis-Speaker-Hooper as the greatest defensive outfield in history, and Major John Hooper has produced uncontroversial statistics in support of this. In longevity, Lewis, now 89, and his deceased teammates, Hooper, 87, and Speaker, 70, average out to 82 years. Note the comparative longevity statistics on selected brilliant outfields, 1880-1922:

	Average Age
Red Sox' 1910-1915 Lewis-Speaker-Hooper	82
Boston Nationals' 1894-1896 Bannon-Duffy-McCarthy	73
Detroit's 1921-1922 Veach-Cobb-Heilmann	62
Philadelphia's 1891-1895 Hamilton-Delahanty-Thompson	57

If you revere statistical hindsight, some interesting speculations can be made. For example, if you could have been born in the year and state of your preference, assuming you would be baseball-oriented, hopeful of a long, useful life, and favoring the period 1901-1911 for your best athletic performances, you would have made these choices: to be born in 1876, exactly 101 years ago, in California or Ohio, or with regional preferences for the Middle West or New England. You also would have offered the early Boston Red Sox the benefit of your abilities, especially as a pitcher. Fred would have been your preferred first name. An analysis of the statistics of the 1901-1911 Red Sox substantiates these hindsight conclusions. But of greater and more practical importance to the reader is an inquiry into the reasons for this significant longevity and its continuing relevancy to the present and future, both for athletes and other people.

It is the author's opinion, based on decades of gathered evidence and evaluation, that Boston Red Sox of the period under study initially adjusted themselves (whether conscious of this or not) at the time of their baseball activity, to accepting life, its stresses and strains and many challenges, sometimes quite unexpected, as gracefully and as undauntedly as possible. This attitude continued upon their retirement from baseball. In a few words, as a group they developed and maintained a competitive and philosophic attitude toward life and its various stages. Extending this concept to the past, present and future, the well-conditioned athlete has certain mental and physical advantages in the happiness and endurance aspects of this human condition, especially when entering middle and old age, difficult milestones for people in general.

There are many factors, some only partially recognized and understood even today, which help to explain why certain individuals and the groups of which they have been a part noticeably outlive people in general. Some of these are: heredity, a rugged constitution, environment, good health practices, domestic happiness, not being accident prone, a certain amount of good luck, avoidance of and resistance to life's most serious diseases from boyhood on, and a healthy, optimistic frame of mind, frequently further aided by religious faith and convictions. Three other relevant factors deserve special identification and comment.

First, these early Red Sox thoroughly enjoyed their occupation, which basically was and still is a game for the young. As Larry Gardner succinctly remarked a few years ago, "We played for fun." Larry also commented on the solidarity of the Red Sox of his era, "In many ways we were a big family." Certainly the implications of his thoughts and words indicate a relation to happy group longevity.

Second, if one accepts the plausible thesis that the association of young people with old people contributes to the longer life span of the latter, the extended baseball careers of many are significant. Retired ball players frequently continue in the sport as coaches or managers of professional teams or as college coaches. Among the early Red Sox eventually achieving very long life, Mitchell, Gardner, Hooper, Wood and Carrigan served as such, while Duffy Lewis was the distinguished traveling secretary of the Boston Braves for many seasons. This youth-association kept them away from their own age group at least for a number of hours each day and thereby conferred a number of advantages, the most useful of which was close contact with youthful attitudes.

Third, former well-known amateur and professional athletes in later years frequently enjoy continued recognition by and friendship with fans after their competitive careers. Boston baseball fans for generations have been nationally recognized for being very loyal and enthusiastic about their heroes for their entire life spans. Call it an ego trip of sorts if you will, but there has been and will be much personal satisfaction as a result of this. Thus, these baseball veterans resist the constrictive, pessimistic thought that age has swept them from the sports scene; rather, they realize that what they have done and tried to do has not been forgotten. As a result, a happy, optimistic and very significant youthful frame of mind has continued, or did continue, in these men, and this is certainly conducive to longer life expectancies.

Fond memories of the old Huntington Avenue Grounds (the original home of the Boston club), their former teammates and respected opponents, and many friendly fans frequently have been conversational and written topics of understandable interest to many of the early Red Sox, including Jimmy Collins, Cy Young, Fred Parent, Norwood Gibson, Jesse Tannehill, Harry Hooper, Joe Wood, Larry Gardner, Duffy Lewis and Bill Carrigan. Early Boston American League baseball has contributed extensive, beneficial influences to many people of different generations, far beyond their immediate ball field attainments.

When the future 1901-1911 Red Sox still were babies, the then American infant mortality rate was appalling because of uncontrolled childhood diseases. A child born in 1876 did well to survive the first few years, as many unfortunates succumbed. When these future Red Sox reached adolescence, they possessed, as a group, healthier-than-average bodies and soon would gain additional benefits from a regimented athletic life: regular routine, good and adequate food, exercise and fresh air, and the several values, both mental and physical, of competition. They avoided the two great American killers of that period, tuberculosis and pneumonia. In later life, the group demonstrated above-average ability and good fortune in avoiding or resisting the onslaughts of the leading killers of recent years—cardiovascular diseases and cancer.

It is a valuable documentary inclusion to quote opinions of two early and great Red Sox, Harry Hooper and Joe Wood, as to the reasons for their own longevity. First, Hooper's, from his letter to the author, dated January 17, 1974:

> Our longevity is due to 2 things, possibly 3. First, inheritance. Both my parents lived to be 94. 2nd to luck. Twice I came near drowning. Had the flu in 1918 when people old and young died like flies. . . . Outside of heredity I think the main way to longer life is diet and exercise.

"Smoky" Joe Wood, in his letter to the author, dated March 26, 1976:

> My mother passed on at 72 years. My father a few months short of 90 yrs. My brother at 84 and my grandparents, on my father's side, were well up in their 80s. From this, one would assume, it is heredity.

Although the author freely admits that heredity is a strong factor, he readily accepts additional ones as being very significant. It is a depressing thought to believe that a person is doomed to a shorter-than-average life chiefly by reason of heredity, obviously an influence beyond an individual's control. But there is no guarantee that heredity alone will insure a long life for anyone. There are, as it philosophically should be, the great influences, to a notable degree the product of self-determination, of what each person does with his or her own mind and body. Therefore, the author believes that the longevity of such as Lewis, Hooper and Wood, also of many others, most probably can be explained as a coordination of heredity, a factor outside their control, and others within their control, such as their individual philosophy and ways of life.

In conclusion, the author selects three factors within personal control. Interested and thoughtful readers are strongly encouraged to reach additional or even different ones.

1. Past history is most useful to mankind when it relates both to the present and probable future. The analyses provided should be helpful both to athletes and many others interested in their own later years and continuing productive lives.
2. Well-trained, experienced athletes, both amateur and professional, should be and frequently are better prepared both mentally and physically for middle and old age and the various challenges such present to mind and body.
3. Especially in New England, and encompassing all Red Sox actives, retirees, and their fans throughout the country and abroad, 1977 is most appropriate to reflect upon and honor the now more complete profile and stature of the early Boston Red Sox. Their individual and team accomplishments by no means have been restricted to winning two pennants, 1903 and 1904, attaining the 1903 World Championship, or creating many records. The multi-faceted and useful Boston durability is a monument in itself. These players, and hopefully many Red Sox of later generations, forever and for many reasons will be a deserved part of Boston history. *Long live the Red Sox!*

MESSAGE TO
BOSTON RED SOX FANS

Vice President and General Manager Dick O'Connell, in his letter to Clark, dated March 20, 1977, very kindly reviewed both the past and prospective future of the Boston Red Sox, since he has been in charge, beginning in 1966:

> We would like to win the World Series in the very near future, as you, yourself, know. As regards the greatest, most pleasing benefit, I might say that it has been very rewarding for me to be with an organization that has shown such a high standard of quality both in baseball and the sports world and also to have been with an owner that has always interested himself in the good of the game and not necessarily that of his own team. He was truly a great sportsman and his objectives have permeated throughout the organization.
>
> RICHARD H. O'CONNELL

* * *

On April 21, 1977, General Manager Dick O'Connell announced that the executors of Mr. Yawkey's estate were offering the Red Sox for sale. Obviously, another change in the trend and pattern of Red Sox history appears imminent, perhaps during the current season, perhaps later. Many prominent names have been mentioned as prospective owners. All loyal and dedicated Red Sox fans agree on two major hopes and desires; the team should remain in Boston and preferably with ownership by competent, enthusiastic local people. These fans also agree on the motto, "**Red Sox Forever.**"

INDEX

(Italic figures refer to illustrations)

Adair, Jerry, 128
Age, ailments of, 124
Agganis, Harry, 104
Agnew, Sam, 45, 48, *94*
Alexander, Dale, 68
Alexander, Grover, 43, *57*
Altrock, Nick, 155
Anderson, George "Sparky," 132
Andrews, Mike, 114, 117
Anthony's Pier 4 restaurant, 123
Arellanes, Frank, 16
Arliss, George, 78
Armbrister, Ed, 131

Baker, Tracy, 28, *51*, 155, 156
Baker Field, 42, 43
Bando, Sal, 128
Barber, Turner, 46
Barberich, Frank, 155, 156
Barnett, Larry, 132, 133
Barrow, Ed, 46, 49, 50, 59, 60, 88, *94*
Barry, Jack, 44
Baseball cards, *24, 25, 26, 91, 93, 96*
Beardon, Gene, 89
Bedient, Hugh, 29, 33, *91*
Bell Gary, 111, 116
Bench, Johnny, 131
Bender, Charles "Chief," *21*
Beniquez, Juan, 129, 132
Berg, Moe, 77
Billingham, Jack, 131, 133
Blue, Vida, 128, 129, 135

Bond, Tommy, 136
Boone, Ike, 68, *97*
BoSox Club, *91*, 123
Boston Cooking School, 148
Boston Herald Advertiser, 113, 134
Boston Red Sox
  brothers on team, 121
  early college graduates, 15
  inventiveness of, 30
  letters to author:
    Burleson, 134-35
    Carrigan, 38
    Criger, 12
    DiMaggio, 82, 85, 86, 87-88, 89
    Doerr, 85
    Ehmke, 66
    Ferriss, 81, 82, 85, 86
    Fisk, 122
    Foster, 41, 124-25
    Gardner, 41
    Gibson, 9, 10, *21*
    Hooper, 12, 17, 32, 38, 40, 50, *54*, 59, 153, 160
    Kasko, 120, *140-41*
    Lee, 151
    Lewis, E., 7
    Lewis, George "Duffy," 17, 18, 30, 31, 37, 38-39, 40, 42-43, *55, 56, 57*, 92
    Lonborg, 112
    Mays, 38, 125
    Monbouquette, 110
    O'Brien, Thomas "Buck," 34

O'Connell, 162
Parent, 9
Parnell, 109-110
Petrocelli, 115
Piersall, 109
Runnels, 109
Schang, 46
Selbach, 9, 31
Stange, 113
Tannehill, 9
Tiant, 151-52
Williams, Ted, 109, 147
Wood, 12, 13, 33, 160
Yastrzemski, 112-13
longevity of, 28, 122-23, 154-61
managers of, 7, 13-14, 33, 35, 36,
       37, 38, 44, 46, 49, 50, 59,
       60, 72, 73, 76, 82, 87-88,
       99, 113, 119-20, 127, 130,
       132, 148
paid attendance, 18, 27, 70, 76,
       78, 87, 111, 117, 137
physical hazards of, 122-23
Press-TV-Radio Guides, 142
teams:
   1901, 6, 155
   1902, 6, 155
   1903, 4, 6, 7, 22, 155, 161
   1904, 4, 6, 7, 8, *21*, 86, 155, 161
   1905-1908, 11, 16, 155
   1909, 16, 155
   1910, 16, 155
   1911, 16, 28, 29, *51*, 122, 155
   1912, 4, 11, 29, 31, 32
   1913, 29, 34, 150
   1914, 35, 36
   1915, 4, 11, 36, 38, 40
   1916, 4, 11, 36, 38, 40
   1917, 43, 44
   1918, 43, 44, 45, *94, 95*
   1919, 43, 49, 50, 59
   1920-1932, 60, 61, 62, 63, 64,
          65, 66, 67, 68, 69-73
   1933-1945, 74-81

   1945-1950, 81-90, 99
   1946, 4, 81-87
   1947, 86, 87, 150
   1948, 88, 89
   1949, 89, 90
   1950, 90, 99
   1951-1956, 99-104, 109, 110
   1957-1966, 104-8, 110
   1967, 4, 110, 111-13, 149
   1968, 110, 115-17, 150
   1969-1974, 117-20, 126
   1975, 4, 126-30
   1976, 126, 134-36, 150
World Series emblems, 1918, 45,
       47, 95
World Series teams:
   1903, 7, *20*, 161
   1912, 31-34, *91*
   1915, 41, 42, 43, *57*, 86, *91, 92*
   1916, 41, 42
   1918, 45-48, *94*
   1946, 83-86, 133
   1967, 113-15, 133
   1975, 130-34
*Boston Red Sox: 75th Anniversary
       History, 1901-1975,* 4, 13,
       156
Boston Red Stockings, 107, 136, 154
Boston Royal Rooters, *91*
Boudreau, Lou, 89, 99
Bradley, Hugh, *25, 92*
Braves Field, 42, 43, *92*
Brecheen, Harry, 84, 85
Bressoud, Ed, 107, 108
Brewer, Tom, 103, 104
Brock, Lou, 114
Bull Durham sign, *51*
Burkett, Jesse, 155
Burleson, Rick, 127, 128, 129, 130,
       131, 132, 134-35, 137, *143*
Burns, George "Tioga," 68, *96*
Burton, Jim, 132
Bush, Joe, 44, 45, 50, 60, 65, *94*

Cady, Forrest, 36, 92
Campaneris, Bert, 128
Campbell, Bill, 135
Carbo, Bernie, 117, 127, 130, 131, 132, *143*
Carens, George, 106
Carlyle, Roy, 68
Carrigan, Bill, 13, 15, 16, *25*, 28, 35, 36, 38, *51*, 72, 88, *91*, 155, 156, 159, 160
Carroll, Clay, 130, 133
Casale, Jerry, 105
Catholic prayer card, 34
Cervantes, Miguel, 110
Chalmers, George, 43, *57*
Chance, Frank, 72
Chandler, Spurgeon "Spud," 79
Chech, Charlie, *24*
Chesbro, Jack, 8, 10
Christian Science Monitor, 4
Cicotte, Eddie, 16, *24*, *25*, 28, 44, *51*, 155
Claflin, Larry, 113, 119
Clemente, Roberto, 114
Cleveland, Reggie, 129, 132, 136, *143*
Clinton, Lu, 107
Cobb, Ty, 38, 39, *55*, 67, 123, 157
Cochran, George, *94*
Coffey, John, *94*
Coleman, Jerry, 90
Collins, Eddie, 75, 76, 100, 106, 109
Collins, Harry "Rip," 65
Collins, Jimmy, 6, 7, 8, 14, *20*, 22, 27, 88, 160
Collins, John "Shano," 72, 73
Collins, Ray, 15, 17, 28, 29, 33, 35, *51*, 92, 124, 156
Concepcion, Dave, 131
Conclusions of book, 148-53
Conigliaro, Billy, 121
Conigliaro, Tony, 108, 111, 116, 118, 121, 122
Conley, Gene, 107

Connolly, Tommy, 41
Cooper, Cecil, 126, 128, 130, 131, 137
Copley Square Hotel, 46
Cramer, Roger "Doc," 75
Crandall, Jim "Doc," 33
Cravath, Clifford "Gabby," 42, 43, 57, 92, 156
Criger, Lou, 6, 7, 8, 12, *19*, 22
Cronin, Joe, 13, 75, 76, 77, 79, 82, 85, 87, 88
Crowley, Bill, ix (Foreword), *142*
Culberson, Leon, 84
Culp, Ray, 116, 117, 118
Curtis, John, 118, 119

Daley, Pat, 13
Darcy, Pat, 131
Dauss, George, 38
Deal, Charlie, 46
Delock, Ike, 104, 105
Devore, John, 33
Dickey, Bill, 79
DiMaggio, Dom, 71, 81, 82, 83, 84, 85, 86, 87, 88, 89, 90, *98*, 101, 102, 103
DiMaggio, Joe, 79, 102
DiMaggio, Vince, 102
Dinneen, Bill, 6, 7, 8, 9, 13, 22
Dobson, Joe, 79, 81, 83, 84, 85, 86, 87
Doerr, Bob, 71, 79, 80, 81, 83, 85, 89, 90, *98*, 100, 101-2
Don Quixote, 110, 115
Donahue, Pat, 156
Donald, Atley, 79
Donovan, Pat "Patsy," 14
Dougherty, Pat, 7, 8, 22
Doyle, Larry, 32, 33, 34, *58*
Doyle, Dennie, 126, 129, 130, 136
Drago, Dick, 127, 128, 129, 130, 131
Dropo, Walt, 90
Dubuc, Jean, 48, *94*
Duff, Joe, 128

Duffy, Hugh, 6, 157
"Duffy's Cliff," 30, *55, 57*

Earnshaw, George, 64
Eastwick, Rawley, 130, 131, 132
Eckert, General William, 47, *95*
Egan, Dave, 106
Ehmke, Howard, 65, 67, 71, 72
El Tiante, 151-52
Ellsworth, Dick, 116, 117
Engle, Clyde, *25, 92*
Evans, Billy, 41
Evans, Dwight "Dewey," 127, 130, 131, 132, 137, *143*

Farrell, Charles "Duke," 22
Fenway Park, 13, 14, 17, 30, 31, 60, 66, 72, 74, 76, 111, 113, 115, 123, 129, 131, 154
Ferrell, Rick, 75, 85, 121
Ferrell, Wes, 75, 85, 121, 123
Ferris, Al "Hobe," 6, 7, 8, 16, *22,* 27
Ferriss, Dave "Boo," 71, 81, 82, 83, 84, 85, 86, 87, 123
Fingers, Rollie, 128, 129, 135
Finley, Charles, 135
Finney, Lou, 75
Fisk, Carlton, 119, 121, 122, 126, 127, 128, 129, 130, 131, 132, 134, 135, 137
Flagstead, Ira, 68, 69, 71
Fletcher, Art, 33
Fohl, Lee, 72
Fornieles, Mike, 105, 107
Foster, George "Rube," 35, 36, *37,* 38, 40, 41, 42, 124, 125
Foxx, Jimmie, 50, 75, 79, 80, 85
Foy, Joe, 108, 111, 117
Frazee, Harry, 39, 43, 44, 49, 50, 60, 61, 62, 70, 71, *94*
Freeman, John "Buck," 6, 7, 8, 22, 27
Frick, Ford, 47, *95*
Fryman, Woody, 118

Galehouse, Denny, 86, 87, 89
Gallagher, Herbert "Dad," *145*
Gardner, Larry, 15, 16, 17, *25,* 27, 28, 29, 32, 34, 36, 41, *51,* *91,* 153, 155, 156, 159, 160
Gaston, Alex, 121
Gaston, Milt, 64, 121
Gavin, Bill, 12, 13
Geronimo, Cesar, 130, 131, 132
Gessler, Harry, 16
Gibson, Bob, 114, 115
Gibson, Norwood, 7, 8, 9, 10, 15, *21,* 22, 156, 160
Glaze, Ralph, 155
Gleason, Harry, 155
God, 152
Golden Rule, 107
Gomez, Vernon, 79
Goodman, Billy, 88, 89, 90, 102, 103, 109
Gordon, Joe, 79
Graver, Larry, *94*
Griffey, Ken, 131, 132, 133
Griffith, Clark, 76
Grinold, Jack, *145*
Grove, Bob, "Lefty," 75, 79, *95,* 123
Gullett, Don, 130, 131, 132
Gunning, Hyland, 28, *51,* 155

Hall, Charles "Sea Lion," 17, *25,* 29, 33, *92*
Harper, Tommy, 119
Harrelson, Ken, 116, 117
Harris, Joe "Moon," 65, 68, *96*
Harris, Joe White, 155
Harris, Maurice "Mickey," 81, 83, 84, 85, 86, 87
Harris, Stanley "Bucky," 76
Harriss, Bill "Slim," 65
Hawaii, 34
Hayden, John, 15
Hemingway, Ernest, 10
Hendryx, Tim, 68

Henrich, Tom, 79
Henricksen, Olaf, *25, 34, 91*
Herman, Billy, 99
Herrmann, August, 48
Heving, Joe, 75, 121
Heving, John, 121
Heydler, John, 48
Higgins, Mike, 13, 82, 85, 99
Hoblitzell, Dick, 35, 36, 44
Holtzman, Ken, 128, 129
Hooper, Harry, 12, 15, 16, 17, *24,*
    25, 27, 28, 29, 30, 31, 32, 33,
    34, 35, 36, 38, 39, 40, 42, 43,
    44, 45, 47, 48, 49, 50, *51, 52,*
    53, 54, 55, 57, *58,* 59, 68, 72,
    92, *94,* 105, 153, 155, 156,
    157, 159, 160, 161
Hooper, Harry, Jr., *58*
Hooper, John, 157
Hoyt, Waite, 60
Huff, George, 14
Hughes, Tom, 7, 8, 22
Hughson, Cecil "Tex," 71, 81, 82,
    83, 85, 86, 87, 123
Hunter, Jim "Catfish," 127
Huntington Avenue Grounds, 4, 6-
    28, 30, *56,* 154, 159
Hurwitz, Hy, 106

"Impossible Dream," 110, 115
Intangible assets, 3, 4, 8, 10, 17, 31,
    32, 79, 111, 112, 136, 148,
    149, 150

Jackson, Reggie, 128
Jacobson, Bill, 68
Janvrin, Hal, 44
Javier, Julian, 114
Jenkins, Ferguson, 123, 134, 135,
    136
Jensen, Jackie, 103, 104, 105, 110
Jesus, 34
Jimmy Fund, 107
Johnson, Ban, 6, 48

Johnson, Darrell, 127, 130, 132, 135,
    136
Johnson, Earl, 86, 87
Johnson, Robert "Bob," 121
Johnson, Roy, 68, 97, 121
Johnson, Walter, 31, *57*
Jones, Dalton, 114
Jones, Fielder, *19*
Jones, Samuel "Sad Sam," 44, 45,
    47, 50, 60, 65, *94*
Jurges, Billy, 99

Karger, Edwin, *24*
Kasko, Eddie, 120, 121, *140, 141*
Kell, George, 102
Keller, Charley, 79
Keltner, Ken, 89
Kiely, Leo, 105
Killilay, Jack, 28, *51,* 156
Kinder, Ellis, 88, 89, 90, 101, 103,
    123
Kinney, Walter, *94*
Kirby, Clay, 131
Kirby, Gene, *96*
Klinger, Bob, 83
Knight, John, 155
Kramer, Jack, 88, 89
Krug, Martin, *91*
Kubiak, Ted, 128
Kuhn, Bowie, 135

LaChance, George "Candy," 7, 22
Lajoie, Larry, 10
Lake, Fred, 14
Lannin, Joseph, 39
Lee, Bill, 118, 119, 127, 131, 132,
    135, 150, 151
Leibold, Harry "Nemo," 68
Leonard, Hubert "Dutch," 35, 36,
    38, 42
Lewis, Ed "Parson," 6, 7, 15
Lewis, George "Duffy," 15, 16, 17,
    18, *25,* 28, 29, 30, 31, 35, 36,
    38, 39, 40, 42, 43, 44, *51,*

54, 55, 56, 57, 91, 155, 156, 157, 159, 160, 161
Lewis-Speaker-Hooper outfield, the 17, 30, 31, 38, 39, *54, 55,* 157
Lieb, Fred, 43, 65
Lipon, John, 102
Lisenbee, Horace "Hod," 64
Lolich, Mickey, 118
Lonborg, Jim, 111, 112, 114, 115, 116, 124
Lord, Harry, 15, 16, *24*
Lyle, Albert "Sparky," 118
Lynn, Fred, 126, 127, 128, 129, 130, 132, 134, 135, 136, *144*

MacArthur, General Douglas, 3
MacFayden, Dean, 64, 65, 71
Mack, Connie, 6, 14, 44, 65, 75
Malzone, Frank, 104, 105
Mann, Les, 47, 48
Mantilla, Felix, 108
Marcin, Joe, 129
Marichal, Juan, 123
Maris, Roger, 114
Marquard, Richard "Rube," 32, 33
Mathewson, Christy, 18, 32, 33, 41
Matterhorn, the, *57*
Maxwell, Charley, 110
Maxwell, Robert, 46
Mayer, Walter, *94*
Mays, Carl, 36, 38, 44, 45, 47, 50, 60, *94,* 124, 125
McAleer, James, 33, 34, 35
McBride, Tom, 84
McCarthy, Joe, 87, 88, 89
McConnell, Ambrose, 15
McDermott, Maury, 101, 102
McEnaney, Will, 130, 131, 133
McGraw, John, 33
McGuire, Jim "Deacon," 14
McHale, Marty, 28, *51, 92,* 155
McInnis, John "Stuffy," 44, 45, 50, 68, 69, *94*

McManus, Marty, 73
Menosky, Mike, 68
Merkle, Fred, 32, 34
Metkovitch, George, 84
Meyers, John "Chief," 32
Miller, Lawrence "Hack," 48, *94*
Mitchell, Fred, 155, 159
Minoso, Minnie, 109
Monbouquette, Bill, 105, 107, 108
Moore, Wilcy, 65
Morehead, Dave, 108
Moret, Roger, 119, 124, 127, 128, 129, 132
Morgan, Harry, 155
Morgan, Joe, 131, 132, 133
Morris, Ed, 65, 66, 67, 97, 124
Moses, Wally, 85
Murphy, Johnny, 79
My Turn At Bat, 82
Myer, Charles "Buddy," 68

Nagle, Walter, 28, *51,* 155
Nagy, Mike, 118
New York Times, 122
Niles, Harry, *24*
Nolan, Gary, 131
No, No, Nanette, 61
Norman, Fred, 131
Northeastern University, 4, *145*
Nunamaker, Les, *92*

O'Brien, John J., 22
O'Brien, Thomas "Buck," 29, 33, 34, *91, 92,* 124
O'Connell, Richard H., 112, 127, 133, *146,* 162
Odom, John "Blue Moon," 128
Official Baseball Guide for 1968, The, 113
Official Baseball Guide for 1970, The, 113, 119
Official Baseball Guide for 1976, The, 113, 129

Oliver, Tom, 69, *97*
O'Neill, Steve, 99
Ostermueller, Fritz, 79
Owens, Brick, 123

Paige, Satchel, 41
Pantages Theater, 42
Pape, Larry, 16, 92
Parent, Fred, 6, 7, 8, 9, 22, 27, 155, 156, 160
Parnell, Mel, 88, 89, 90, 101, 102, 104, 108, 109
Pattin, Marty, 119
Pennock, Herb, 50, 60, 65
Perez, Tony, 132
Pertica, Bill, *94*
Pesky, John, 81, 83, 84, 87, 89, 90, 99, 101
Peters, Gary, 118
Petrocelli, Rico, 111, 115, 117, 118, 127, 129, 130, 131, 132, 136
Pick, Charlie, 46
Piersall, Jimmy, 102, 104, 108, 109
Pipgras, George, 60
Pitching hazards
    ball park, 123, 124
    other places, 66-67, 124
Pole, Jim, 123
Popowski, Eddie, 120
Powers, Mike, *21*
Pratt, Derrill, 68
Prothro, Jim "Doc," 68
Putnam House, 12

Quinn, Jack, 65, *96*, 124
Quinn, Robert "Bob," 61, 62, 67, 70, 71, 72, 73

Radatz, Dick, 107, 108
Raschi, Vic, 90
Reach's 1913 Guide, 34
Reach's 1919 Guide, 45, 46, 153
Rhyne, Hal, 69
Rice, Jim, 126, 127, 136, *144*

Richards, Paul, 123
Riggert, Joe, 28, *51*, 155
Rigney, Emory, 68, 69
Rixey, Eppa J., 43, *57*
Rolfe, Bob "Red," 79
Romo, Joe, 128
Romo, Leon "Red," 128
Rose, Pete, 130, 131
Roth, Bob "Braggo," 59
Rothrock, Jack, 68
Rudi, Joe, 128, 135
Ruffing, Charles "Red," 65, 67, 71, 79
Runnels, Jim "Pete," 105, 107, 108, 109
Ruppert, Jacob, 50, 60, 61
Russell, Glen, 84, 85
Ruth, George H. "Babe," 35, 36, 37, 42, 44, 45, 49, 50, 59, 60, *94*, 123, 124, 153

Saint Anthony, 122
Santiago, Jose, 111, 114, 116, 123
Scarritt, Russ, 68
Schang, Wally, 44, 45, 46, 50, 60, 68, *94*
Schilling, Charles, 107
Schwall, Don, 107
Scott, Everett, 36, 44, 59, 60, 69, 93, *94*
Scott, George, 111, 116, 117
Selbach, Albert "Kip," 8, 9, 31, 155
Shakespeare, William, 62
Shanks, Howard, 65
Shaw, Al, 155
Shean, Dave, 44, 45, 48, *94*
Shore, Ernie, 35, 36, 37, 42, 44
Shotton, Burt, 13
Siebert, Wilfred "Sonny," 118
Slaughter, Enos, 84, 85
Smith, Reggie, 111, 115, 117, 118
Snodgrass, Fred, 34
Somers, Charles, 6
Spalding, Albert, 107

Speaker, Tris, 16, 17, *24*, *25*, *26*, 27, 29, 31, 32, 34, 35, 36, 38, 39, 54, 55, 57, 92, 157

Sporting News, 14, 113, 135

Stahl, Charles "Chick," 6, 7, 8, 12, 14, *20*, *22*, 27, 35, 121, 124

Stahl, Garland "Jake," 15, 16, *22* *23*, *24*, 29, 32, 33, 35, *56*, 92, 121

Stange, Lee, 111, 113, 116, 117

Steele, Elmer, 156

Stephens, Vern, 89, 90, 101

Stevens, Mark, 4, 7

Strunk, Amos,4 4, 45, 69, *94*

Stuart, Dick, 108

Sullivan, Frank, 103, 104, 105

Sweeney, Bill, 69

Tabor, Jim, 79

Tangible assets, 5, 79, 112, 148, 149, 150

Tannehill, Jesse, 8, 9, 13, 16, 156, 160

Taylor, John I., 12, 14, *52*, *53*

Tebbetts, George "Birdie," 99

Tenace, Gene, 128

Tesrau, Charles "Jeff," 32, 33

Thomas, Fred, 36, 48, *91*

Tiant, Luis, 118, 119, 123, 127, 128, 129, 130, 131, 132, 135, 136, *144*, 151, 152

Tiant, Maria, 152

Tobacco cards, *24*, *25*

Tobin, John, 68

Todt, Phil, 69, *96*

Unglaub, Bob, 14

Vache, Ernie, 68

Vernon, Jim "Mickey," 104

Village, the, 12

Volz, Jacob, 155, *156*

Vosmik, Joe, 79

Waddell, George "Rube," 10

Wagner, Charles "Heinie," 16, 24, 27, 29, 33, 59, 72, *91*, *94*

Wagner, Charlie, 79

Wagner, Hal, 81

Walker, Harry, 84, 85

Wall, Murray, 105

Walters, Al, 50, 59

Wambsganss, Bill, 68

Washington, Claudell, 129

Waslewski, Gary, 115

Webb, Earl, 68

Webb, Mel, 106

Wertz, Vic, 105

Whales, 151

White, Sam, 102

Whiteman, George, 44, 45, 46, 48, *93*, *94*, 153

Williams, Dick, 112, 113, 119, 147

Williams, Ken, 68

Williams, Ted, 71,, 79, 80, 81, 82, 83, 85, 87, 89, 90, 99, 100, 101, 102, 103, 104, 105, 106, 107, 108, 109, *139*, 147

Willoughby, Jim, 127, 135, 136

Wilson, Earl, 107

Wilson, Jack, 79

Winslow, Palmer, 70

Winter, George, 7, 15, *22*

Wise, Rick, 123, 127, 128, 130, 131, 136, *144*

Witt, Lawton "Whitey," 65

Wolter, Harry, 155

Wood, Joe, 12, 13, 16, 17, 23, *24*, *25*, 28, 29, 31, 32, 33, 34, 36, 37, 39, *51*, 86, *92*, 123, 155, 159, 160, 161

Wright, George, 107, 154

Wright, Harry, 107

Wyatt, John, 111, 115

Wynn, Early, 110

Yastrzemski, Carl 27, 31, 80, 107, 108, 111, 112, 113, 114, 115, 116, 117, 118, 119, 127, 128, 129, 130, 131, 132, 134, 137, *139*, 147

Yawkey, Thomas A., 47, *57*, 71, 74, 75, 76, 78, 87, 88, 104, 106, 112, 133, 134, 138, *146*, 147, 162

Yerkes, Steve, 17, *25*, 28, 33, *51*, *91*, 156

York, Rudy, 82, 83, 84, 85, 87

Youmans, Vincent, 61

Young, Denton "Cy," 6, 7, 8, 9, 10, 11, 12, 13, 16, *19*, 22, *24*, 105, 111, 124, 155, 156, 160

Zarilla, Al, 90

Zimmer, Don, 27, 136